GHOST WALKS IN AND AROUND BAKEWELL

TEN WALKS THAT REVEAL THE SPECTRAL SECRETS OF BAKEWELL AND THE SURROUNDING AREA

JILL ARMITAGE

COUNTRY BOOKS

Published by Country Books/Ashridge Press
Courtyard Cottage, Little Longstone, Bakewell, Derbyshire DE45 1NN
Tel: 01629 640670
e-mail: dickrichardson@country-books.co.uk

ISBN 978-1-906789-21-3

© 2009 Jill Armitage

British Library Cataloguing in Publication Data.
A catalogue record for this book is available from the British Library.

By the same author

IN THE PARANORMAL GENRE:
HAUNTED PLACES OF DERBYSHIRE
GHOST PETS & SPIRIT ANIMALS
THE HAUNTS OF ROBIN HOOD
ROMANTIC HAUNTS OF DERBYSHIRE
HAUNTED DERBYSHIRE
HAUNTED PEAK DISTRICT

WALKING BOOKS:
DISCOVER THE AMBER VALLEY

Printed and bound in England by Digital Book Print Ltd
Tel: 01908 377084

CONTENTS

INTRODUCTION

If you enjoy a relaxed approach to walking, why not come with us and discover some of the best 'haunts' of the area. These are leisurely strolls rather than arduous hikes or robust rambles, visiting some of the areas best loved beauty spots like Bakewell, Chatsworth Park, Lathkill and Monsal Dale. We delve into their history, their claims to fame and folklore, and uncover some fantastically spooky stories.

Ghost Walks In and Around Bakewell is a book for enjoyment and recreation based upon ten walks that take you deep into the places where people have seen ghosts, heard them and, most frightening of all, felt them. These places with their hidden secrets and surprises are closer than you might think and all the walks offer suggestions for escape routes if the going gets tough or too scary.

Varying in length from one mile to ten, the shorter walks are ideal for an afternoon stroll, an evening amble or, for extra atmosphere wait until its really dark – if you dare! They make a surprise and interesting addition to a hen night or Halloween celebration – shivery, spooky fun guaranteed to raise the spirits on cold dark nights.

Jill Armitage
2009

The sketch maps that accompany each walk are for general guidance. Along with the instructions, they should be quite adequate, but for back up, if you decide to take a diversion or join two walks together, take an Ordnance Survey Explorer, formerly OS Outdoor Leisure Map 24.

1: A Ghostly Legacy

BAKEWELL TOWN CENTRE GHOST WALK
Distance – 1 Mile (1·60km)

Bakewell is often referred to as the Gateway to the Peak. It is the largest and most important town within the boundaries of the Peak District National Park and attracts thousands of visitors, drawn by its scenic beauty, its array of interesting shops and the opportunity to sample a genuine Bakewell pudding. It's a place you never tire of, but if you want a new experience to fill a leisurely hour wandering around Bakewell, this is the walk for you. Steeped in history and with a strong paranormal past, Bakewell is something of a psychic hotspot, so why not join us on our Bakewell Ghost Walk? This walk has two distinctions. It is the shortest walk in the book but has the most 'ghost stops' – a vast and varied selection of 20.

It's ideal for a Sunday afternoon stroll, an evening amble or for extra atmosphere wait until its really dark – it you dare! The Bakewell town centre walk is ideal to incorporate into your Halloween celebrations or hen night frivolities, but most of all, its an enjoyable walk with a new and exciting twist.

Bakewell lies astride the A6 Derby-Buxton road at its junction with the A619 and B5055. Park in any of the town centre, pay and display car parks, or on Monday which is market day, use the Agricultural Centre Car Park. All are sign posted on the main routes into the town.

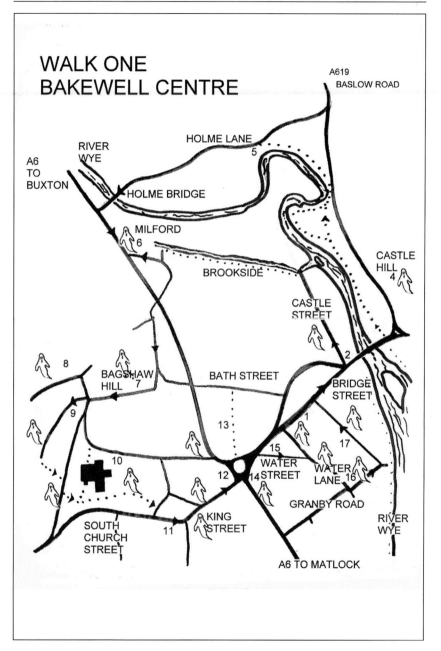

THE BAKEWELL TOWN CENTRE WALK

Our ghost walk begins and ends at the Old Market Hall – 1, now the Information Centre a prominent building in the centre of the town with a large adjoining car park. Built in the latter half of the 17th century, the Old Market Hall originally had open arches on the ground floor to protect the market traders from the weather. It has been used for a variety of purposes. In 1827 it was the Town Hall; later the ground floor was a wash-house and the first floor a court room. In 1891 it was a restaurant, and chip shop. Later it became a rating office, dance hall, and library.

Bridge Street and arket Place c1910 with the 17th century Old Market Hall – now the Tourist Information Centre – in the centre, being used for commercial purposes. The shops on the left have been left with a ghostly legacy.

Bakewell is renowned for its market and is the principle centre for the north midlands. The first recorded reference to a market charter here is in 1254 when a weekly market and a 15 day fair was granted to the Lord of the Manor, William Gernon. In 1330, Bakewell became a market town and has continued to prosper ever since The cattle market was moved from the town centre a few years ago to a purpose built cattle market across the river, but locals still occasionally hear the sound of ghostly cattle mooing in the night.

Go to the entrance of the Information Centre and with your back to the doors, turn to the building on your left. This block with its protruding ground floor shops was built in the 17th century by a pharmacist named John Denman. Could it be his ghost who is still hanging around?

One of these shops was occupied for a long period in the mid 1900s by Dunn's chemist and the people working there had many strange experiences including seeing a ghostly shadow and objects moving. Taken over by Boots chemist prior to moving into their present premises, their staff also experienced ghostly happenings. The most bizarre was the chair that moved. This was a courtesy chair supplied for the use of customers while waiting for their prescriptions to be made up, but every morning, the chair was found in a different position to the one in which it had been left the previous evening. One day while attempting to leave the dispensary, a pharmacist found the door held fast. It couldn't have been locked, but he could not get out. One of the assistants found the chair had been jammed under the door handle and no one in the shop had done it.

At one time this block was a girl's school and some people have reported seeing a woman they describe as an old style governess walking down the stairs that lead out into the street. While decorating, a man heard footsteps going up these stairs and as no one was supposed to be in the building, he went to investigate. The place was empty but as he hadn't heard anyone leave, he felt very perplexed. He sat on the bottom step and waited. After a few moments he heard the footsteps walking back down the stairs. He turned but there was no-one there and the footsteps passed straight through him.

The window of Stewarts shop dressed for Hallowe'en, but the genuine ghosts still make themselves known in this block

Turn back to the Old Market Hall and veer left past the building to walk away from the town along Bridge Street. At the junction on the left is The Castle Hotel – 2. This old hostelry was formerly The Roebuck, and stands on the corner of Castle Street, built in the late 18th century.

George, a former resident of Castle Street was woken regularly by the sound of horses walking up and down the street. This became such a regular occurrence that on one occasion waking in a grumpy mood he decided to give the early morning equestrian a piece of his mind. He leapt out of bed, drew back the curtains and opened the window, but instead of seeing a horse and rider the entire street was deserted and the sound had simply gone. That evening, George related this story after a few drinks in the bar of The Smithy Inn and was told that up to a century ago, the horse market had been held outside the Castle Hotel and the horses exercised along Castle Street. So had George somehow tuned into the sound of ghostly horses being trotted along this road?

We all rely upon our senses to interpret everyday happening whether they are sounds, sights or smells, but sometimes they are templates out of which all manner of things can be moulded by the human mind, bending reality to fit human expectation and suggestibility. If George had known about the horses being exercised down Castle Street we could accept this as the solution but he didnt. Unknown to him, he had heard a complete repeat of an actual incident that occurred regularly many years ago, an event imprinted like a time recording in the ether.

Horse fairs were held outside the Castle Hotel in the years before World War I, but they have left a ghostly legacy

*The Castle &
Commercial Hotel
in the mid 1880's –
Humphrey Davy
Hudson, proprietor,
stands in the doorway
with two of his
daughters in front*

For a shorter town walk that doesn't go through the water meadows or over the old packhorse bridge, turn left along Castle Street and at the end, turn left to follow the footpath by the side of the mill stream to the Victoria Corn Mill – 6 – where we meet the longer walk.

The famous medieval bridge over the River Wye is an artist's delight

The longer walk continues over the famous medieval bridge – 3 – that straddles the River Wye and still carries all the town's traffic on the A619. This picturesque bridge with its five pointed arches was built about 1300, widened in the 19th century and has been in constant use for 700 years.

Follow the road round to the left. Ahead of you is Castle Hill – 4.

The first mention of Bakewell comes from 920AD when Edward the Elder, the ruler of Wessex, built a burgh or fortress against the invading Danes on what is now Castle Hill. The Anglo Saxon chronicle records the building of it at a place known as Badecean Wiellon, meaning Beadeca's Well, from which today's name Bakewell is derived.

Castle Hill House is an elegant Georgian construction that sits on the slope of Castle Hill. It was built in 1785 for Alexander Bossley, a Bakewell attorney who died unmarried in 1826. The house then passed to his cousin John Barker, a Sheffield lead merchant. He rented it out for a period before selling to the Duke of Rutland who used it initially as the residence of his agent. It had a continuous run of tenants until in the post war period it became a country club, before being sold to the County Council for use as a boarding house for Lady Manner's School until 2005. At some time in its chequered past, a rather tragic incident occurred that has left paranormal activity in its wake.

Castle Hill House, the haunt of Jim the butler

Jim Marlow was a butler at Castle Hill House, but Jim was finding life unbearable and one day he flipped. He left the butler's pantry closing the door behind him, walked along the corridor and up a flight of stairs to the gun-room where he selected a suitable gun then returned to the pantry where he locked the door behind him. A few minutes later, there was a loud bang and Jim Marlowe had shot himself.

This sad incident happened on a Friday evening and apparently, every Friday evening since, if you listen carefully you will hear Jim Marlowe re-enact his last walk from the pantry to the gun-room. There is a loose floor board at the entrance to this room and it is heard to creak ominously under the weight of the phantom's footstep.

Almost opposite Castle Hill House, go through the gate in the stone wall on your left into the water meadows and follow the path upstream until reaching Holme Lane – 5. Turn left and follow this to Holme Bridge where you are able to cross the River Wye. Note the low sides which indicate that this was an old packhorse bridge. At only 1·25 metres wide, the very low parapet prevented the loaded panniers carried by the horses from catching the stone sides as they crossed the bridge. It was rebuilt in 1664 with the steeply humped crossing which allowed for floodwater. When tolls were charged for all goods

The narrow pack horse bridge was just wide enough to allow loaded pack horses to cross

crossing Bakewell Bridge, Holme Bridge was used as an alternative route to avoid the tolls, and the path we are following is an old pack-horse route used by the pack-horse trains and to drive stock cross-country. A packhorse train would consist of 40-50 horses. They wore down the track and helped by the rain, the ways became deeper and deeper and were known as hollow ways. This is often reflected in place names like Old Hollow Plantation just north of Bakewell.

The River Wye and the water powered industry along its banks has played a major part in the town's story and this area, once cluttered with mills is called Millford.

Walk over the bridge and straight ahead until meeting the A6 Buxton Road. Turn left heading towards the town, and Victoria Mill – 6 is the three storey gritstone building 30 metres on your left. Here the shorter walk will join in.

Victoria mill is believed to have been built on the site of the original Bakewell corn mill listed in the 1086 Domesday Book and valued at 10s 8d (approximately 53 pence). This building probably dates from the mid-nineteenth century. Up to the end of World War Two the mill was used by the local farmers for grinding corn. The mill wheel 16ft diameter x 14ft wide was driven by the waters of the River Wye until 1960. It was then removed and the old and decaying water wheel can be seen in its yard.

The old mill wheel has been left to rot in the yard of Victoria Mill

14

The boys from St Anselm's school regularly passed this mill and dared each other to hang around. They say that an old miller haunts the place and looking at it's gloomy façade it's not difficult to believe that he actually does.

Cross the road and turn right up Bagshaw Hill – 7, one of the steepest climbs you will encounter. Half way up the hill is Bagshaw Hall, built on the site of the former Moor Hall, parts of which could date back to the early 16th century and possibly earlier.

Bagshaw Hall was Thomas Bagshaw's pride and joy and not only did he give the hall his name, to show off his new hall, he invited all the local dignitaries to a feast to enable them to admire his new abode. Amongst those that attended was the Duke of Rutland who reminded the host that as the land on which the house was built was actually part of the Rutland estate,

Bagshaw Hall has a ghost in the attic

by rights he could legally take possession of any building on his land. The comment may have been made in jest but Thomas Bagshaw took it very seriously. According to legend, he was so distraught at the thought of loosing his beautiful hall, he went into the attic, threw a rope over the beam and hanged himself. Ever since his ghost is said to wander the attic.

Over the years, the property has been a private residence, the Conservative Club, an office complex and is now in the process of being converted into luxury residential and holiday lets. While an office complex, a courier making a delivery couldnt get out quick enough after sensing the ghost. Recently one lady who lived there as a child admitted that they never played in the attic because of the strange feeling up there.

When one owner threw a party, in order to accommodate all his guests overnight, he and his wife planned to sleep in the attic. He was moving bedding up the stairs when he saw the ghostly figure of a man. Naturally this rather unnerved him but he decided to pass it off as an illusion and didnt mention it to his wife. That night she woke up screaming after feeling the sudden heavy weight of something on her legs. Sitting on the bed was a ghostly man. She shot down the stairs, leaving her husband to collect up the bedding, and they moved permanently out of the attic.

Continue up Bagshaw Hill until reaching an unmarked cross roads with North Church Street. Look over to your right and through the gate you will see the grounds of St Anselms Prep School – 8.

St Anselm's School was founded by Mr William Storrs Fox in 1888 on its present site of 18 acres. The main school buildings are accessed by continuing up this road which becomes Stanedge Road, but our story features a phantom photograph taken in the garden. Apparently a garden party was taking place and one of the masters was taking photographs to record the occasion. When the photographs were processed (pre-digital days) one group standing on the garden steps had been joined by another figure, a boy in Victorian dress.

Proceed straight ahead into Cunningham Place – 9 and over to your right is The Old House Museum. This intriguing old house is one of the oldest surviving domestic properties in the Peak. It was built as a parsonage house in the reign of Henry VIII and the first written record dates from 1534. It has been a private dwelling house, a farmhouse and a tenement block but by 1954 it was condemned as unfit for human habitation. Just before the bulldozers moved in, it was saved by the newly formed Bakewell and District Historical Society who have restored and conserved the building.

Has the ghost of Bakewell Museum been caught on camera?

A visit to the Old House Museum is highly recommended, not just to enjoy a fascinating look at the various aspects of past social life in and around Bakewell, you could also experience some ghostly activity. One of the staff told me that things in everyday use often go missing. At one time she mislaid' an item of stationery she knew had been left on a shelf in her office. Would you mind returning that item were you found it?' she asked the empty room. Next morning it was back on the shelf.

The museum is ably manned by a dedicated group of volunteers. One of the ladies told me that she was upstairs sorting through some things when she heard the front door open and footsteps walking along the stone floor. This surprised her as she knew the door was locked and she was in the building on her own. Because of the gaps between the floor boards, it is possible to see through from the first floor down to the ground floor, and she peered through the cracks to see who could possibly have entered. She called, but there was no reply. The room was empty but unconvinced she went downstairs to check. Despite a thorough search, she was alone. Others will tell similar stories but all are in agreement that the spirits of the Old House Museum are not malign. Members of various paranormal groups have spent the night at the Old House Museum but despite elaborate procedures have found nothing specific. That is not to say that the place does not possess a resident spirit or two, it definitely does.

Leave the Old House Museum and turn right. Walk across to what appears to be a dead end where in the far left corner you will find a footpath that leads down to Church Lane. Almost ahead of you is the lych gate of the church

One evening two local guys were taking a short cut through the churchyard. They were just about to proceed up the hill when ahead of them standing by the lych gate they noticed a man dressed in black. He began to glide towards them and they stared in horror because although he wore a tall hat which seemed to give him extra height his feet were missing. This would indicate that he was actually walking on the old path which prior to being tarmaced, would have been lower in his time.

The bulk of the Church of All Saints – 10 now dates from the 13th and 14th centuries with considerable 19th century restoration, yet there has been a Christian church on this site for over a thousand years. Although nothing remains except a hint of Norman superimposed on

Saxon work, a considerable collection of 9th and 10th century masonry and carved stones can be seen on display inside the church and the porch. And don't miss the ancient stone coffins propped up by the south-west corner. With the shape of human figures hewn into the stone, these make a good photo opportunity – if you dare!

Children pose in the stone sarcophagi outside Bakewell Church

The inside of the church has some fine and interesting artefacts, and the south transept houses the Vernon Chapel, a Victorian reconstruction with a pair of huge wall monuments at either end. One is to Sir George and Lady Margaret Vernon of Haddon Hall, and the other to their daughter Dorothy and John Manners. Haddon Hall is still owned by Dorothy and John's descendants. *See Walk 2.*

In the graveyard you will find an 8th century Saxon cross with a ghostly tale which dates back to 1501 when the cross was positioned just north of Bakewell. Prince Arthur, the eldest son and heir apparent of Henry VII (1485-1509) was betrothed at the age of twelve to Catherine, the fourth daughter of Ferdinand, King of Castile and Aragon. The marriage had been arranged by proxy at the chapel of Bewdley Manor and one of the witnesses to the contract was Sir Henry Vernon of Haddon Hall. Sir Henry was Arthur's governor and treasurer, and the young prince was a frequent visitor at Haddon Hall.

One day in September 1501, as Prince Arthur sat by the cross deep in thought, a vision materialised from the cross. Described by one writer as a tall, thin female dressed in white, her features sunken and wan, her lips of ashy hew, and her eyeballs protruding, bright and motionless, the wraith stared at Prince Arthur for several minutes, then slowly raising her arm she said –

'Unhappy royal Prince, mourn not thy fate which is not thine! One earthly pageant awaits thee, yea, it is at hand; and then, ah! Then thou will drop into the lap of thy mother – ah thy mother earth! Forth comes to Britain's shore thy lovely smiling bride – ah! bride and widow of a royal boy!'

Deeply disturbed by such a vivid prediction, he was mulling over the meaning of such words of doom as he returned to Haddon, where he was greeted with the news that his bride had arrived from Spain. His orders were to return to London immediately, and there he was to be married with all the pomp and ceremony such an occasion deserved. The first part of the prophecy had come true.

Arthur and Katherine were married and moved into their new marital home, Ludlow Castle in Shropshire, but after only four months Prince Arthur became seriously ill. With no chance of recovery, on his death bed, the last words spoken by the young prince were said to have been Oh, the vision by the cross at Haddon!'

Wayside crosses, where itinerate priests and monks would preach when in the area, were removed and destroyed by an Act of Parliament in 1643. All crosses in public places had to go, but many local citizens circumvented the wishes of parliament by concealing these crosses with the intention of re-erecting them when the government policy changed, which it was likely to do at short notice during the Civil War. Like this cross in the churchyard at Bakewell, others can be found at Eyam, Hope and Chapel.

The Saxon cross in the graveyard

Leaving the Saxon Cross, proceed down the path through the churchyard until coming out on South Church Street – 11 As you walk towards the town it becomes King Street.

> Across the road is Cadcliffe House, the old Job Centre and now once again a private house. This attractive Georgian House is a fine example of the town houses built in the mid eighteenth century by the industrialists and merchants of Bakewell, reflecting the wealth generated by the industrial revolution. Apparently people have seen the ghostly form of a Georgian lady waiting at the door of Cadcliffe House but no sooner has the fact registered than she simply melts away.

On your left is the Old Town Hall, a most pleasing 17th century building with mullioned windows. When functioning as a town hall, there had been a holding cell under the steps, but over the years this had been blocked up. The building has since housed a school, a working men's institute, the town's fire engine, note the bell on the top used to summon the fire-engine, a fish shop, an antique shop and various others. One recent owner asked a local builder to open up the holding cell to make a store room. He began work but after a while came to the floor which seemed rather high. He dug deeper and found the skeleton of a woman built into the wall. Her identity and how she came to be there is still a mystery.

The butter market where farmers wives could sell their produce was held in front of the Old Town Hall, and this was also the site of the Bakewell riots which followed the passing of the Militia Act, which from 1796 led to the quarter sessions no longer being held in Bakewell.

The village stocks were also positioned here. Stocks were not introduced into English law until 1351 but by a statute of 1405, any village without a set of stocks could be downgraded to a hamlet. Those who refused to obey the law could be put in the stocks for all manner of petty crimes. In the 17th century, a further amendment was added to the already existing list of crimes punishable by a period in the stocks – 'Any person convicted of drunkenness should be fined 5s or spend six hours in the stocks'. In 1703, a James Cozier of Bakewell wilfully broke the stocks; his sentence was to occupy them as soon as they were repaired.

This is the start of the shopping centre. Bakewell is a busy market town, with some interesting shops, many of which are haunted. To list them all would be repetitive because what they all appear to have in common is that strange things happen when there are changes to the displays or when a property is being revamped or refurbished. As one proprietor told me; 'Its as if someone or something likes to just let us know that we are being watched, or checked..... keeping us on our toes.'

Turn to your left and go under the archway into King's Court, a delightful oasis courtyard. Previously Avenel Court, it was the rear yard of Michael Goldstone's Antique Shop which specialised in early period furniture and decoration. The old buildings in the courtyard were sympathetically styled to give a medieval look to complement the antiques.

People in the street have seen a face at this window,
but this time, it's only a mask – I think!

With a change of usage, Avenel Court was opened up to a number of smaller businesses and these changes obviously activated spirit activity. The Pink Elizabethan looking building was an ice-cream parlour but on numerous occasions the entire stock was spoilt when the electrical supply to the freezers was found inexplicably turned off. The proprietors had no option but to move out.

Plugs have also been mysteriously unplugged and electrics malfunction at J.R's Brasserie which is also the haunt of a grey man. The kitchen where much of the activity occurs is upstairs. People in the street have seen a face at an upstairs window and staff in the room below have heard the sound of someone moving around when there was no-one there.

There has been much speculation as to where the Bakewell witches lived and the most obvious place, where most of the houses of the period were congregated, would be in this area just below the church, here in this charming courtyard. The Youth drama group used this as a setting to put on a play about the Bakewell witches and said it was very spooky especially when a black cat walked along the ridge of the roof and a bat flew out.

These two so-called witches ran a milliners business in Bakewell in the early 1600š, and took lodgers to supplement their income. One nameless Scottish lodger refused to pay and in desperation Mrs Stafford threw him out, keeping his clothes for security.

When found in a cellar in London in just a tattered nightshirt, the Scotsman was taken before a magistrate on suspicion of being concealed in an unoccupied room for sinister purposes.

He was asked; "Where are your clothes?"

"They are at Mrs Staffordš house in Bakewell, Derbyshire," replied the wary Scotsman.

"Have you walked from there with only a shirt torn to ribbons on your back?" his Worship asked.

"How I came here, I dont know, twas like a wind; but Mrs Stafford came the same fashion. I was in bed at three očlock this morning at Bakewell, when through a crack in the floorboards, I perceived Mrs Stafford and her accomplice preparing for a journey. I heard Mrs Stafford say – over thick, over thin, now devil to the cellar in Lunnun. Immediately they disappeared and all was dark."

The lodger thoughtlessly repeated the words but changed över' to through; then at the last word, a rush of wind passed through the room, carrying him away in his nightclothes. A moment later, he found himself all tattered and torn, sitting next to Mrs Stafford and her companion in a lamp-lit cellar in London. The women were tying up parcels of silk and muslin which they had obviously purloined from the shops in the metropolis. Mrs Stafford offered him wine, he drank and fell fast asleep. When he woke, the women had gone.

The magistrate took down his depositions, and decided that this was a clear case of witchcraft. He ordered the accused witches to be seized and conveyed to the county gaol with the suggestion that they should be tried on the manš evidence and executed immediately. They were hanged as witches in 1608, but do their troubled spirits still roam around their old home?

Belief in witchcraft was a major element in community life and a large part of the witch's stock in trade were charms and potions. Around the beginning of the 17th century when Ellen Gregory of Over Haddon went to seek the advice of John Rowlandson, Vicar of Bakewell, she showed him a bag that hung from string round her neck. Inside the bag was a slip of paper with about ten lines written on it. It was intended as a charm, hung there by a witch who had been paid by her husband to cure what he considered was her insanity. (*see Monsal Witches Walk 9*)

This medieval-style building is haunted, but could it be the Bakewell witches?

The stereotype image of a witch

Continue down King Street until reaching Rutland Square – 12, the busy central hub of Bakewell where all the roads meet.

Seeing the phenomenal success of Buxton Spa re-instigated by his aristocratic neighbour the Duke of Devonshire of Chatsworth House, The Duke of Rutland, from nearby Haddon Hall decided that Bakewell should get in on the action. He built a Bath House with a bath which measured 33ft x 16ft utilizing the waters of the Great Well in the Bath Gardens – 13 – over to your left across the roundabout.

He filled the bath with Chalybeate spring water, named the Bath Gardens the Botanical Gardens and in 1804, orchestrated the building of the Rutland Hotel on the site of the former White Horse Inn to accommodate all the expected visitors.

He built opulent Georgian terraces like the Rutland Terrace, and other fine houses on the A61 Buxton Road, one of which we once owned or rather shared with a former occupier who hadn't moved on. As I have no wish to alarm the current occupiers, it would be unfair to name the actual house which has now been divided, but if you think it could be your house, do get in touch.

We bought the house at auction for £13,000 which even in 1978 was ludicrously cheap for a town house in Bakewell. It had been occupied by an old lady who had died there. After removing all saleable contents, and before it could be put on the market the estate agent had filled five skips with rubbish. It was completely uninhabitable and in places unsafe. Like most of the woodwork, the stairs were rotten and we had the constant fear of the floor giving way and everyone being pitched into the cellar. All this had obviously put off many potential buyers and we anticipated months of building work but the problem was, we couldnt keep builders. Contractors would start with great enthusiasm then down tools and disappear without any notice or reason.

I had sensed some form of ghostly presence right from the beginning, but tried to convince myself that it was my imagination. I never saw anything that couldnt in all sincerity be blamed on my imagination, but it was regular to experience sudden cold spots, a tingling, tickling sensation on my skin and sounds that could not be accounted for. People laughed when I voiced my concerns, but after a number of frightening experiences, no one could convince me that one particular room didnt hold some malignant force. Years later, my mother who is a complete non-believer admitted that shed felt 'spooked' there on numerous occasions too.

Eventually we found a Sheffield company who actually got down to work and at last we were making progress, until the two guys who had been constantly on the job for a few weeks decided to quit. I refused to pay them until they told me why.

Its this place. It gives you the creeps,'they confessed. Its as if someone is always watching you. We've felt someone breathing down our necks, a cold hand on ours, icy cold draughts and weird noises. Things are moved, items disappear and reappear days later in different places.'I knew they were not exaggerating. I had experienced all that and more. The last straw was when one of the guys went to buy sandwiches for lunch. He hadnt been gone long when his colleague heard him return and thinking hed forgotten something waited for him to enter the room. The footsteps grew nearer, the door opened then closed but there was no-one there. Not only did they quit, so did we; we sold the property and never went back.

Peakland water is regarded as special but Bakewell was always overshadowed by Buxton only fifteen miles away by turnpike. Unrelated to the amount of rain fall, the volume of Bakewell water varied considerably, so to compensate, bore holes were driven to improve the water supply. Sadly nothing could be done about the temperature which, at a constant 53 degrees F. was a lot cooler than Buxton water, pleasanter to drink but not to bathe in. There was a further chalybeate well known as Peat Well, (probably a corruption of St Peter's Well) with waters at 56 degrees F on the east side of Matlock Road, (see Walk 10), and although plans were also made to exploit this spring as a spa nothing came of that venture either. By 1820 the town had piped water by courtesy of the Duke of Rutland's Haddon estate. The building which housed the bath was bought in 1909 to use as extra premises for the 6th form and staff of Lady Manner's School (see Walk 2). In more recent years it has been used by the British Legion and is now a private house named Haig House.

Only the Rutland Arms Hotel still hints at the optimistic hopes of once turning Bakewell into a Spa town. It can boast of the fact that many famous people have stayed there including Jane Austen whose stay inspired her to write Pride & Prejudice. But the Rutland Arms Hotel is best known for the happy accident that happened in the kitchen and produced the Bakewell Pudding for which Bakewell is now known world-wide. We can't guarantee that you will smell any-thing quite that delicious, but many hotel guests regularly report the

The Rutland Hotel was built to impress the thousands of visitors
the Duke of Rutland expected to take the waters of Bakewell

smell of tobacco smoke which is now even more obvious after the smoking ban.

Cross the road to the impressive Jacobean style building that at one time was R. Orme & Co – high class grocers, later John Sinclair Ltd., specialist in fine china and crystal, and is now the Edinburgh Wool Shop.

In the 1990s when John Sinclair Ltd occupied the building, they had a warehouse on the top floor. One night after closing, two stockmen went up in the lift and as the lift doors opened they stared in horror as a grey man walked across the floor ahead of them. Others that have seen him say he is only half a man. He is cut off somewhere around knee height which would indicate that he is walking on a different floor level. This would suggest that this spectre could be from the earlier building that occupied the site and was demolished in 1936-38. Our photograph shows that this building did in fact have different floor levels to the building that replaced it.

The left side of Bakewell Square facing King Street around the turn of last century. The Rutland Arms is to the right. The building on the left houses Critchlow's butcher's shop, Fred Allens Drapery and Haberdashery, the Bakewell Clothing Hall, a drapery and clothing business that had been in existance since 1747, and C. A. May photgrapher. Note the differet floor levels of the three storey building which houses R. Orme & Co. This building was demolished in 1936-38 and a new building erected, but it retained its resident ghost

*Rutland Square looking towards Bridge Street. The ornamental lamp in
Rutland Square was erected in 1897 to honour Queen Victoria's Diamond Jubilee.
On the middle right is the Red Lion and the Post Office faces the oncoming traffic*

At the end of this block turn right and walk down Water Street – 15
– which runs into Water Lane. About thirty years ago half way along
Water Lane was a sweet shop run by an old lady with a distinctive
limp. Is it possible that she could still be around?

A man was walking along Water Street one evening and ahead of him was
an old woman stumbling along and leaning heavily on a stick. He followed
her until she reached the door of a shop where she simply vanished. The
logical explanation would be that she'd gone into the shop but her inability
to move easily and quickly, and the door step made that highly improbable.
Recounting this strange event later, we realised that the shop was the
original sweet shop and his description of the old lady fitted that of the
previous owner.

During the 70s, 80s and 90s, the end block facing you which is now
shops and offices was The Smithy Inn – 16, owned by my family. It was
through this association that I learnt of many Bakewell paranormal
activities and a few actually happened to me. Part of the Smithy Inn,
as its name would imply had been the old whitesmith's forge on the
side of the market. It had been in existence since the early nineteenth
century specialising in wrought iron work for both farming and
household use. Although most of the Smithy Inn was a new build, it
still had paranormal activity.

The Smithy Inn was built on the site of the old smithy on the south side of the market

A period stage coach from Red House Stables waits outside the Smithy Inn

All the fourteen bed-rooms were en suite and for security reasons all rooms were automatically kept locked. When occupied each guest took possession of their own key, but we could never account for how one room had all the signs of being occupied without any evidence of a guest, at least not a physical one! The bed never looked rumpled but in the bathroom, the towels, normally neatly folded were often found crumpled on the floor and damp. There was never any evidence that the shower or the wash basin had been used, not even an odd water droplet, yet there were often signs of condensation on the windows.

There was one room in the old part of the Smithy Inn that always seemed to have a distinctive smell. It wasnt unpleasant or particularly strong but it was persistent and could not be accounted for. Initially I thought it was the furniture polish used by the previous owners, but when we changed suppliers and produce, the smell still remained. I probably wouldnt have thought anything more about it if I hadnt read a postcard being sent by a guest staying in that room.

Let me just assure you that I was not in the habit of reading postcards deposited at the reception desk for posting, so how I came to read this particular one is rather uncertain. It was probably placed deliberately on the desk with the 'staying in a haunted hotel' underlined specifically so that I would see it.

Obviously I had to say something although I was surprised that the visitors hadnt. When they returned later that day I took the opportunity to ask whether everything was to their satisfaction and how they liked Bakewell. They smiled and assured me that everything was fine. Bakewell was a most interesting place and the countryside delightful.

'And is your room satisfactory?' I asked. I wasnt sure whether I detected a slight hesitation before they assured me it was. Apart from admitting that I had read their postcard I couldnt do a lot more, so we parted company.

It wasnt until they were leaving that they confided that they hadnt wanted to cause a fuss, but they had often been aware of a strong scent of something like honeysuckle, and the lady had woken one night to see a young woman feverishly searching through a set of drawers which in the cold light of day had no physical existence.

'Why didnt you say something,' I exclaimed in mild shock. 'We could have moved you to another room.'

'Oh no dear,' the lady exclaimed, 'the room was more than satisfactory. It is a lovely room and felt so homely. Whoever that young lady was she had obviously been happy here.'

Turn left into Granby Road, then left again into Market Street and you are in the car park – 17 where ahead of you is the Information Centre which marks the start and end of our Bakewell Ghost Walk. But just before the end of the walk, pause to look at the building on your right. You may be tempted to go inside because this is the Peacock Public House.

A barman at The Peacock went down the cellar and when he tried to return, found the door had mysteriously jammed. He banged and shouted, but despite there being many people in the public bar no-one could hear him. He tried his mobile phone but couldnt get a signal. Eventually he managed to climb up the barrel chute. As he walked in through the door, people looked at him in surprise and asked where he'd been. When he told his story, they went to check the cellar door and found it opened easily and there was no means of locking or blocking the door. At other times, staff have found the beer taps turned on or off in the cellar, and three men standing at the bar saw a ghostly figure in the doorway.

The old stables adjoining the Peacock have now been converted into holiday lets. Last summer, one group of guests staying there, explained to staff that they hadnt locked the rooms because they had left the maid in there. The staff looked puzzled. There was definitely no maid that fitted the description of a lady wearing a long dark dress with a full white apron over.

No visit to Bakewell would be complete without sampling a genuine Bakewell Pudding. There are at least three shops selling this delicacy and numerous cafes, pubs and hotels dotted around the centre. There is also a special delivery service so it is possible to send one to friends in far away places.

Could this be the ghost of Mrs Greaves who mistakenly made the first Bakewell Pudding? Regretably no – the mannequin stands in the window of the Original Bakewell Pudding Shop

2: A Spitting Spectere, Fasting Damsel and Frock-coated Phantom

BAKEWELL – HADDON – OVER HADDON
Distance 6 Miles (9·75km)

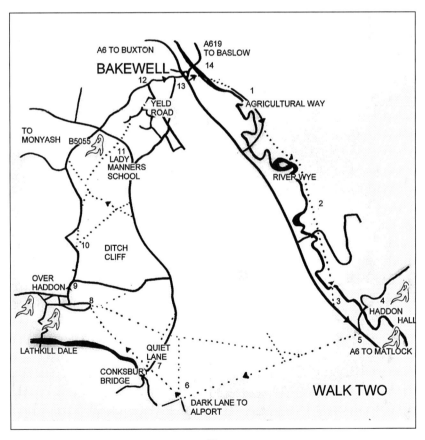

This leisurely walk with at least six ghostly encounters, follows the route of the River Wye down-stream to Haddon Hall, a perfectly pre-served Mediaeval Manor House and home of the Dukes of Rutland. Allow yourself at least a couple of hours to appreciate the splendours of Haddon Hall. It is open April to October and at Christmas, but check the times with Bakewell Tourist Information Centre (01629 813227) when planning your visit.

Walk up Haddon Fields and stroll through quiet, unspoilt country-side before wandering along the stunningly beautiful Lathkill Dale to reach Over Haddon, and back to Bakewell. This is a circular walk which starts and ends at the pay and display car park at the Agricultural Centre Bakewell SK221:684. From the centre of Bakewell take the A6 south and after ½ mile the Agricultural Way is sign posted to your left.

The inscription on the Roman altar found in Haddon Fields in 1698

THE WALK

Leave the car park and walk south, back along the Agricultural Way – 1 – until the road bends to the right. Keep straight on along the footpath, following the fence and trees close on your left. Cross the stile and continue ahead, following the hedge on your left and river on your right. The path goes steadily on while the river continues to come and go in convolutions. Cross a foot-bridge to follow the river side path through a belt of trees, over the stile at the end of the wood and after a while, bear left up the bank above the river.

In 1698, a Roman altar made from gritstone was found in the fields on the level valley floor between Bakewell and Haddon – 2. The altar is now in the entrance porch to the banqueting Room at Haddon Hall. The stone dates back to about 150AD and the translated inscription upon it reads – "To the god Mars Braciaca, Quintas Sittius Casecilianus, Prefect of the First Cohort of the Aquitanians, performs his vow."

After about 1 mile, pass through a gate and turn right down a lane. After about 30 metres turn left over a metal stile. Continue on this riverside path through what can be gooey woods, crossing a bridge over the Wye, then follow the path to cross a stile onto the A6. The land on your left are the grounds of Haddon Hall, but note the stone building over to your left – 3. This is a rare example of a pigeon house dating from an age before refrigeration when fresh meat in winter was in very short supply. Fresh pigeon was a welcome addition to a diet of salted or dried meat.

In the trees to your left rising on the limestone slope above the River Wye you might just catch a glimpse of Haddon Hall – 4. A traveller who visited in 1697 described it as a 'good old house', because even then, the hall had 600 years of growth and history behind it. Succeeding generations of its owners, Peverel and Avenel, Vernon and Manners had from the 12th century onwards built, enlarged and improved until the original modest hall became a picturesque array of towers, turrets and battlemented walls.

In the early 18th century, Haddon ceased to be occupied and so it escaped the wholesale rebuilding which many great houses under-went in the Georgian period. Last century the 9th Duke of Rutland decided to arrest the process of romantic decay, restore the hall and make Haddon his main home. This was done with such care, skill and attention to detail that today Haddon is unrivalled in this country as a perfectly preserved medieval great house.

It is highly advisable to break your journey here.

The entrance to Haddon Hall c1911

The cottage and entrance tower in 1918 before the mid 1920's restoration

The formal gardens at Haddon

The paranormal activity at Haddon Hall is neither well documented nor encouraged, yet there is definitely something that even the sceptics cant fail to notice. People who work at Haddon testify to a friendly, homely atmosphere and yet find it difficult to discount the ghostly activities. The eeriness of the surroundings, combined with draughts and possible crepitation of ancient timber, and their effect on the imagination, might well suggest phantom footsteps, creaking stairs and gently closing doors. On the other hand, the sounds may be the genuine creation of some super-natural presence.

While on fire-watching duties at the Hall during the second world war, one employee heard strange and mysterious noises during his lonely vigil and attributed these to some ghostly intruder from the past. Members of staff have frequently heard footsteps in various places in the empty hall and the head steward has experienced a presence while she was locking up.

One visitor apparently witnessed a spectral cook in the kitchen beating a young kitchen lad, and another visitor said her twelve year old grandson who had accompanied her on a visit, felt so oppressed by presences, he simply couldnt walk through the long gallery.

An ex-comptroller heard female voices and laughter in the courtyard and author Joan Foreman recorded in her book The Mask of Time how she had passed through the courtyard at Haddon and seen a group of children playing at the top of some steps. She vividly recalled one girl aged about nine who wore a Dutch-style hat which covered her shoulder length hair, and a distinctive long, green/grey dress with a lace collar. The writer clearly saw the girls face but as she moved forward the vision melted into thin air.

Perhaps the most amazing experience happened to one of the staff about twenty years ago. He had just walked through the banqueting hall and started to climb the dog-leg stairs to the Long Gallery when he stopped in mid-stride. There, ahead of him at the top of the stairs was a woman in a dark Elizabethan dress, yet she was not a living, breathing woman, this was a fully formed ghost. As he stood transfixed, she rolled a gobbet of phlegm round in her mouth and spat it on the floor, a habit we now find quite disgusting but which would have been quite acceptable in Elizabethan society. Taking a few seconds to compose himself, the man turned and ran. The experience had left him badly shaken and he retired shortly afterwards.

An estate worker was convinced that he had seen the spectre of Dorothy Vernon, the heiress of Sir George Vernon who in the mid 16th century defied her father and eloped. The story of her elopement has been dubbed Derbyshires Most Dramatic Historical Romance. Despite the elopement, Dorothy Vernon was not disinherited and her marriage to John Manners started a dynasty.

On my many visits to Haddon Hall, I am always drawn to the death mask of Lady Grace Manners in the small museum. Lady Manners was the founder of the school in Bakewell which bears her name, and which we will pass later in this walk. She was also the daughter-in-law of Dorothy Vernon, the eloping heiress. After psychometrising, I feel that it is this Lady Manners who is often in visitation at the Hall and the probable spitting spectre.

On leaving Haddon Hall – 4, cross the road and join the footpath to the right of the Haddon Hall Car Park – 5. Go through the gate at the side, into a field and follow the stony bridleway uphill keeping the field boundaries on your left to cross three large fields. In the third field pass the farm and at the junction of paths go through a gate in the field corner.

Alternatively, on your left is Dark Lane – 6 which leads to Alport in case you wish to combine this walk with the *Middleton – Youlgreave – Alport Walk 3*.

To continue our walk, bear very slightly right across the next field towards Conksbury Bridge. Cross the stile and keep straight on aiming for the stile to the left of a field gap. Cross Quiet Lane – 7, the Bakewell/Youlgreave Road just above Conksbury Bridge

Quiet Lane signs stand on either side of Conksbury Bridge and on Moor Lane in Youlgreave. They were erected in 2003 in a pilot scheme by the Countryside Agency to establish a countrywide network of peaceful, rural lanes. The signs are to encourage motorists to cut their speeds and be extra vigilant for the safety of walkers, cyclists and horse riders sharing the same route.

On the other side of the road is another stile. Squeeze through and keep straight on to cross a double stile.

Quiet Lane

Crossing the Bakewell/Youlgreave road then a stile towards Over Haddon

The path now stays above the eastern section of the Lathkill River. Cross a fence stile and bear left up the field. Cross a stile and go through a small gate and continue up hill towards Over Haddon – 8. Head for the white building in the distance at the right hand end of Over Haddon village – the Lathkill Hotel.

The quiet hamlet of Over Haddon on its rocky prominence over-looking Lathkill Dale is an ideal centre for walkers and anglers, but on at least two occasions in the past, it was the centre of much controversy.

In the mid 17th century Martha Taylor's inedia stunned the medical profession. Inedia is the alleged ability to live without food indefinitely or for extreme periods of time. Many religions have a long established tradition of fasting as a spiritual practice for the purification of the body and mind, but Martha Taylor was a simple lead miner's daughter, born at Over Haddon in February 1651.

The first ten years of Martha Taylor's life were perfectly normal then she was accidentally knocked in the back by a neighbour. Shortly afterwards paralysis set in, and she was confined to bed. Despite a year of inactivity she ate well and for a brief period in May 1662 her paralysis subsided. Sadly this didnt last and for the next five years, poor Martha was confined to bed permanently paralysed.

In September 1667, sixteen year old Martha began to experience many strange and frightening occurrences. Tears of blood ran down her face. She began to hiccup so loudly she was often heard three doors away. Despite eating very little, she was perpetually being violently sick, her body was wracked with pain, cramp and convulsions. Everyone feared that death was near as Martha lost her voice then fell unconscious. She stayed like that for two weeks then unbelievably she regained consciousness. From then on she refused to eat. Even the tiniest morsels caused her to wretch violently. The only nourishment she had was an odd raison. Infrequently she asked for wine or milk, not to drink, but to moisten her lips.

As the weeks passed, news of these unusual circumstances began to circulate as far a field as London and teams of learned physicians, scholars and professors came to see and investigate this unusual phenomenon. To make sure there was nothing deceptive a rota of 40-50 local women was drawn up so that there were always two of them in Martha's room at any time keeping watch.

The public began to take a keen interest and pamphlets were written to keep the public informed of the latest developments.

During this fast, many things happened to Martha Taylor. She once went without sleep for five weeks. She temporarily went deaf. If well wishes sent her flowers which were put in her room, she would say they were too strong for her brain.

Thanks to the publicity we know that her fast continued for a year but what happened then is unsure. The only concrete evidence is in the Bakewell Parish Register where her burial is entered on June 12th 1684. This would indicate that Martha lived another sixteen years and died at the age of thirty three.

The second incident was totally different yet no less remarkable.

Derbyshire has always been a county rich in natural resources. Underneath its sculptured hills and valleys lie a honeycomb of old lead mine workings but image the impact caused in 1854 when a piece of iron pyrite thought to be gold was discovered in an old lead mine at Manor Farm, Over Haddon. As the news spread it brought chaos, crowds and feverish speculation to this peaceful, totally unspoilt area noted for its isolation and solitude. The Lathkill gold-rush was underway.

The Over Haddon Gold and Silver Company was formed to extract the ore, and plans were made to build a railway to Over Haddon from Bakewell to transport the precious metal. Shares sold fast, then the gold was discovered to be of the fools variety, so the whole enterprise came to a crashing halt. Now all that is left in those old sealed-off mines are the ghosts. In those subterranean depths we are left with a legacy of ghostly stories and sightings of old miners who shouldnt be there.

Like many people working in hazardous conditions, miners were very superstitious. No one was allowed to whistle down a mine because it was believed that the sound drove the ore away. It was not unusual for miners to leave shoes and small clay pipes known as fairy pipes in mines for good luck and if a piece of machinery wasnt working, it was quite normal to cover it in a protective layer of branches from the Rowan tree or Mountain Ash which was and still is considered to be an anti-witch tree. This was done in the belief that the power of the tree would counteract the witchcraft which the miners believed had stopped the machinery working.

Walk down the road in front of the Lathkill Hotel and on your right in the dip you will find the old village pump which is also the site of one of Over Haddon's well-dressings. It would also be advisable to look out for a frock-coated phantom, who was last seen walking down the road towards Lathkill Dale in our next ghostly story. In contrast, the only strange encounter I had was with the Green Man, depicted here in one of the Over Haddon well-dressings.

A rather unusual and very striking well dressing depicting the Green Man,
a character from folk lore

An Over Haddon lead miner's daughter named Martha Taylor
went without food for a year

39

When Mr Denham obtained a job at the D.P Battery works, the former Lumsdale Mill at Bakewell, he and his wife looked around the area for somewhere to live, and their search ended when they found a pretty cottage snugly situated on the slopes of the lovely Lathkill Dale with delightful views over the surrounding countryside. The Denhams couldnt believe their luck at finding such a delightful place and made an offer which was accepted almost immediately.

Very soon they moved in with all their possessions but found that somehow they were not able to create the atmosphere of cosiness and comfort that the cottage had initially suggested. There was nothing tangible, just a feeling of uneasiness. Although she saw nothing unusual, Mrs Denham often sensed a malignant presence inside the cottage, while Mr Denham and two nephews regularly saw an elderly gentleman in a top hat and frock coat enter through the gate of the terraced garden and walk along the stone flagged path to disappear at the cottage door.

Mrs Denham was unable to see him, but as an early warning device, she fastened tin cans to the gate. Every time anyone opened the gate, the tins rattled and clattered, but when the phantom visitor entered, the cans remained silent. He was so real to the two boys, they sometimes amused themselves by shooting arrows or throwing orange peel to try to dislodge his tall hat.

They called the spectre, the frock-coated phantom and Mrs Denham discussed the possibility of an exorcism with the local preacher. He suggested that the spectre may be caused because the man had died in unusual circumstances and never received a Christian burial. He advised that on the next appearance of the restless spirit, the burial service should be read to terminate his wanderings.

A little while after this, Mrs Denham was alone in the cottage when she heard a noise that she recognised as the lifting of the door latch. She distinctly heard someone enter, and thinking it was her husband, went to greet him but the room was empty. Her heart began to pound and she was gripped by sudden fear, but remembering what the preacher had advised, she quickly picked up her book of Common Prayer and began to read – I am the resurrection and the life saith the Lord; he that believeth in me, though he be dead, yet shall he live; and whosoever liveth and believeth in me, shall never die. We brought nothing into this world and it is certain we can carry nothing out. The Lord gave and the Lord has taken away; Blessed be the name of the Lord.'

Suddenly the room seemed to have a distinct stillness and she no longer felt afraid. She walked over to the door, opened it wide and walked outside. A neighbour who was just passing had stopped and was staring in stunned disbelief. I've just seen a gentleman dressed in period clothes leave your cottage and walk down the road towards Lathkill Dale,' she informed Mrs Denham.

They both looked in the direction the neighbour indicated but the frock coated phantom had disappeared.

Take the right fork uphill to join School Lane then turn right at the road junction to Bakewell Road – 9. Leave Over Haddon and proceed along this road, ignoring the road to the right and the track to the left, for nearly ½ mile. Where the road bends to the left, go through the squeeze stile straight ahead – 10. Walk down the steep slope to cross a gated stile. Turn right to walk towards and past the footpath post and follow the path as it gradually descends to the valley bottom.

Follow the path on your left, cross a broken wall, down the valley until you reach a gated stile on your left. Go through the gate and turn left.

Walk up the field following a wall now on your right. Pass through a squeeze stile in the field corner. Keep straight on. A wall is now on your left. As you near the field corner, turn right to walk towards old stone gate-posts. Follow the hedge on your left.

Cross the stile in the field corner. Turn left in a few yards, then turn right to follow the hedge on your left. Cross the stile in the field corner. Keep straight on passing the grounds of Lady Manner's School on your right – 11 – to arrive at Shutts Lane.

The foundation stone of Lady Manners School was laid by the Duke of Rutland on May 20th 1936 on the 300th anniversary of the founding of the original school by Grace Lady Manners who we have just encountered at Haddon Hall. According to the deeds, when Lady Manners opened her school for local boys on May 20th 1636, she instructed that the school master should be unmarried. He was to work from 7 a.m to 11 a.m and from 1 p.m. to 5 p.m, read prayers at the parish church every morning at 6 a.m between Lady Day and Michaelmas and at 7.30 a.m at other times. For this he received £15 per annum, the money being the rent charge for four fields at Elton. Initially Lady Manners School shared accomodation with the older Chantry School in South Church Street before moving in 1826 round the corner to the Old Town Hall, King Street where it remained until 1874.

The footpath runs by the side of Lady Manners School

Some years ago, a local lady recounted a story which happened to her and a school friend while they were playing in Lady Manners School Yard. They heard the sound of galloping horses and indistinct cries coming closer as if travelling along Shutts Lane. The horses' hooves came nearer then there was the report of a pistol as the sound travelled past the yard, yet there was nothing to be seen. A minute later came another clash of hooves, going in the same direction but again there was nothing to see. It was a frightening experience for the two young girls and one they would never forget. They always believed that they had experienced a Civil War skirmish three hundred years after the event. Were the eager Round-heads in hot pursuit of hapless Cavaliers?

The footpath narrows as it begins to fall down into the town

The view from the footpath as it falls down towards Bakewell

Cross the road and walk down the well defined path that runs alongside the tennis courts and playing fields. The path is hard surface and well lit. As the houses start, go through a couple of kissing gates and keep straight on past a small children's playing area on your left. Walk along the pavement for a short distance before crossing Highfield Drive to follow the path as it continues directly ahead between the houses. The path narrows as it begins to fall gradually down and the church becomes visible straight ahead before opening out into the Yeld. Where the road bears right, carry straight on down steps to Yeld Road.

One evening, the Reverend Thomas Lomas was returning from Bakewell to his home in Monyash, but apparently in the darkness, he lost his way and he and his horse fell over the Parsons Tor in Lathkill Dale. For many years the tuft of grass found in his clenched fist was preserved in a glass jar in Monyash Church and many people have seen the figure of the spectral clergyman standing in the church. Poems have been written on this local epic.

43

Turn right down Monyash Road which runs into King Street. After passing the Parish church and the almshouses on your left you will reach the old Town Hall the ground floor of which housed Lady Manner's School between 1826 and 1874. Pass the shops to reach Rutland Square – 13. Turn right into Matlock Street, and cross the A6 at the official crossing. Turn right, then left into Granby Road. Proceed to the bend where it becomes Market Street – 14, and turn right to cross the river. The Agricultural Centre Car Park which is the start/end of this walk is straight ahead.

The view of All Saints Church, Bakewell, from Yeld Road c1900

3: A Phantom Coach, Deathly Duel & Heartless Knight

MIDDLETON – YOULGREAVE – ALPORT
Distance 2¼ Miles (3.65km)

This is a leisurely stroll rather than a hike so that you can appreciate seven ghostly tales, and the historical charm and paranormal activity of three quaint, upland villages in the heart of fine limestone scenery, linked by the beautiful Bradford Dale.

This walk is a half and half. We suggest that you leave your car in Alport and catch the Hulleys 171/181 bus to Middleton village, the terminus of the bus service that runs every two hours or one hourly at weekends. Check the times with Bakewell Tourist Information Centre (01629 813227) when planning your walk.

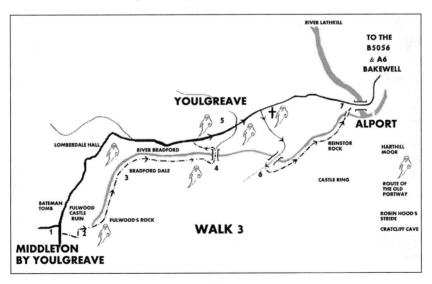

To reach Alport from Bakewell, take the A6 south and just after passing Haddon Hall, take the B5056 on your right. The road runs for just under one mile alongside the River Lathkill, after which you take the turning to your right, sign posted to Youlgreave. After ¾ mile you will reach Alport. Turn left off the main road and park.

Alport stands at the junction of the Lathkill and Bradford Dales and played an important role as the river crossing point on the Portway, a pre-historic track-way that stretched north to south through the heart of the Peak District linking important trade, cultural and spiritual sites – see also *Walk 6 & 10*.

The quiet village of Alport was once a major river crossing point

The river was the source of power for the former village corn mill, and old cottages cluster by the water, but undoubtedly there was a settlement here, pre-Roman times. There was certainly an Iron Age hill fort known as Castle Ring – SK222:628 – just south of here along the Portway track, and the remains of a Bronze Age stone circle on Harthill Moor – SK226:627 – known as the Nine Stones although only four of the nine stones now remain upright. Understandably these sites have a distinct atmosphere and a few paranormal stories.

A few years ago, a farm labourer working on Harthill Moor found a tiny clay pipe called a fairy pipe. These tiny pipes were sold complete with tobacco as a sort of sample to be smoked just once. They were often left in the old lead mines by superstitious miners as an offering to placate the spirit that inhabited the mine and was held responsible for any casualties or un-explained incidents occurring in or around it.

According to our story, this farm labourer smoked the fairy pipe and began to hallucinate. The ground opened up and he saw 100's of small, fairy people gaily dressed and enjoying themselves.

The realm of the fairies supposedly impinges on that of humans, but is rarely glimpsed unless by accident, invitation or abduction. Certain trees, particularly the oak, hawthorn and ash are believed to be sacred to fairies and anyone who falls asleep under such a tree is likely to be under fairy influence or might even get carried off by the little people. On the other hand, our farm labourer may have been under the hallucinogenic effect of certain species of fungi, so if you intend to pick wild mushrooms on your walk, do take care and if in doubt leave them or you might be away with the fairies too.

Just off the Portway further south is a rock outcrop known as Robin Hood's Stride and next to it is a small hermitage at the base of Cratcliffe Tors SK227:623, This is not a deep cave, and hewn in the rock is a crucifix some four feet high, a niche for a lamp and a couch. According to records at Haddon Hall, it was occupied by a hermit who preached to travellers along the Portway in the 16th century, although historians believe this was a much older practice.

A late 12th century carving of a traveller carrying a staff and pouch, n Youlgreave Church. It probably represents a pilgrim that walked the Portway

47

THE WALK

Our walk begins and ends at Alport although the first part is a bus ride. Leave the car near Alport Bridge which dates from the 18th century, and walk back to the main road where the bus to Middleton will stop on demand. While you are waiting, look for the notice attached to the side of Alport Barn. According to the 1824 Vagrancy Act – *'All vagabonds found lodging or begging within this hamlet will be taken up and dealt with as the law directs'*.

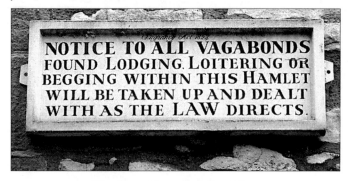

The sign on the wall of Alport Barn

Catch the bus at Alport which takes you through Youlgreave where the road is narrow and parking is at a premium. Drivers are forced to follow a series of chicanes around a plethora of stationary vehicles.

Leaving Youlgreave on the road to Middleton, watch out! These are typical country roads, hardly wide enough for vehicles to pass, yet there are other hazards too.

This is the road that is frequented by a phantom coach. According to Clarence Daniels in his 1975 edition of *Haunted Derbyshire*, he was told by Mrs H Johnson of Winster that her father – a local game keeper – was compelled to press close against a wall as a coach and eight horses thundered past him at Roughwood Hollow, between Youlgreave and Middleton. This phantom coach was so real, he actually felt a strong draught as the horses and vehicle went sweeping past. Others have also reported seeing the coach at night when it is lit by flickering lamps and accompanied by ghostly dogs.

Could this phantom coach be that of the local squire Thomas Bateman? He purchased Middleton Hall and estate at the end of the 18th century and had the hall completely rebuilt in local gritstone. He is also responsible for rebuilding the whole village of Middleton – 1 – in the 1820s, incorporating gritstone details and mullioned windows into limestone buildings to retain a traditional appearance. The village pub on the square was the Bateman's Arms. Sadly it closed it's doors 50 years ago and is now a private house named Square House. Middleton now has no pub, shop or café. It's just a quiet agricultural backwater set among beautiful rolling hills and limestone dales at the very heart of the White Peak, but it has quite a history..

Before reaching Middleton and half way along the Youlgreave/Middleton road, you might catch a glimpse of Lomberdale Hall on your right, built in 1844 by another Thomas Bateman, grandson of the aforementioned Thomas. This Thomas was the well-known archaeologist who during his short life is said to have examined over 500 ancient burial mounds or barrows around the Peak District. In 1856, he enlarged his home to house his growing collection which included a significant number of valuable Bronze Age artefacts, now housed at Sheffield City Museum.

At his death in 1861, aged only 39, Thomas Bateman was buried in the grounds of the Congregational Chapel built by his grandfather in 1826 (now a private house/holiday let) and where at the age of four, he had laid the foundation stone. Thomas Bateman's tomb can be reached along a rather overgrown, sign posted path next to the former

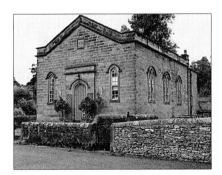 

The former congregational chapel behind which is Thomas Bateman's impressive tomb

chapel. It is surrounded by iron railings and surmounted by a stone replica of a Bronze Age cinerary urn.

To begin our walk, leave the hamlet of Middleton – 1 along a surfaced road opposite the small recreation area. It descends gently and loses its surface. Take the footpath, sign posted on the left.

The roads of Middleton are safe enough for the geese to use

In the early 1600's, two hundred years before the Batemans came to Middleton, Sir George Fulwood built a fortified manor house known as Fulwood or Middleton Castle here. It's now long gone, but at the time it was described as an embattled house of great magnitude.

Sir George's son Sir Christopher Fulwood was a staunch Royalist who gave his life for the cause during the Civil War. In the Autumn of 1643 Sir Christopher mustered together 1,100 Derbyshire men, mainly local lead miners to march to Derby in support of the King. In retaliation, on November 13th 1643, Sir John Gell sent a strong force of parliamentarian soldiers to ransack Fulwood Castle. Sir Christopher was shot but in a desperate attempt to escape, he hid behind a large rock at the head of Bradford Dale, known locally as Fulwood's rock. Sadly he was cornered and taken prisoner but his wounds proved fatal and he died on his way to Lichfield gaol.

Fulwood Castle fell into disuse after the Civil War and after eighty years was demolished. The stone was re-used in building Castle Farm and other village houses, and all that now remains, besides the mention in the ordnance survey maps, are barely visible, grassy mounds behind Castle Farm which hide traces of limestone walls and foundations.

As we continue our walk, there are soon rock faces on either side, forming a mini dale – 2. At the bottom of the slope, the track bears to the left along the bottom of the well-wooded Bradford Dale, but the stream usually has very little water in this section. When you reach a bridge with a junction of footpaths, go straight on, through a gate and follow the footpath with the river over to your left. This section is a series of dams and ponds known as Bradford dams, an area teeming with fish and wildfowl – 3.

Those of a sensitive nature may detect an atmosphere that hangs heavy in the air around here. Although I have not come across any ghostly sightings, the trauma of the past is all around Fulwood's Rock where Sir Christopher Fulwood of Fulwood Castle made his last desperate stand against those roundheads.

In addition, some 200 years later in 1820, a skeleton was found in a field between Youlgreave and Middleton by Youlgreave. The skull had been smashed in, but was believed to be the remains of a Scottish or Jewish peddler murdered 70 years previously.

After about ¾ mile go through a gate and cross the river over an ancient clapper bridge – 4. This is one of the earliest forms of bridges supported on piles of stones sunk into the river bed and spanned by massive stone slabs.

The ancient clapper bridge over the River Bradford

On your right, immediately after the clapper bridge is a five bar gate and a squeeze stile with a Limestone Way sign post. It might be appropriate here to explain that some of these stiles are slabs of encrinitial limestone, also known as Derbyshire Marble. They are polished smooth by the clothing and footwear of those who have squeezed through them to use the footpath. And while on the subject of stiles, they are not called squeeze stiles for nothing; the narrowness of these stiles is to stop sheep straying from their pastures, but its hard luck if you have a sturdy walking companion or dog. I know! I had a portly Labrador called Flint.

If you don't want to visit Youlgreave continue on this path by the side of the river until reaching the old pack horse bridge. To visit Youlgreave – 5 – ignore the broad Holywell Lane, and turn left to follow the footpath as it rises steeply up the hill. Ahead of you are the lead miners cottages, now converted into desirable residences, and this would have been the well trodden route the lead miners would have taken from the mines across the other side of the valley back home. This could also be the setting of our next ghost story.

The steep path up to Youlgreave used by the old lead miners

A miner was excavating fluorspar at a mineral outcrop at Wenley Hill, Youlgreave. It was a lonely job so one day on his way to work when he encountered an old man, the miner invited him to join him while he worked.

Where are you working?'asked the old man.

Wenley Hill,'said the miner.

Not likely lad. Ah'm not coming up theer. It's haunted.'

The miner laughed and tried to assure the old man that it was not. But the old man insisted he knew of the appearance of a headless dog, sinister influences and uncanny happenings. He also pointed out the uncanny stillness and lack of bird song in the area, then to back this up, he told the miner a story. One day, he and his brother had been walking along Wenley Hill to attend to some cattle at farm buildings in the corner of a nearby field. As they walked, the figure of a man appeared and preceded them along the lane. Then just as suddenly, he disappeared. Both men had witnessed this and also, more surprisingly, they both agreed that the man was headless.

As you wind up between the cottages, you will come out on Bankside opposite the Methodist Chapel, Youlgreave. This climb is the most testing section on the route.

Maps, road signs and guide books seem unable to agree on how to spell the name of this Peakland village, which is often spelt as it is pronounced Youlgrave. The fact that it was once an important lead mining centre could be the clue to the original name as grove/groove is a local word for a lead mine. Lead miners were often known as groovers. Could Youlgreave be derived from 'Youl's grove', a lead mine belonging to a man named Youl? Alternatively the Youl could be derived from yellow, the colour found in the local rock – possibly baryte or barium sulphate.

It's quite a relief after the steep climb from the dale to find that the long main street of Youlgreave – 5 – which runs along the ridge that separates Lathkill Dale from Bradford Dale is virtually flat. Turn right and walk towards the centre.

Youlgreave retains an old-world feel, partially because it is largely devoid of pavements and is totally free of disfiguring yellow lines. A pedestrian route is marked on the road but take care.

This main street must rank as one of the most attractive street scapes in the Peak District with its rows of simple stone cottages, punctuated by some distinctive individual buildings. On your left is the Farmyard Inn, originally a farmhouse until it became an inn two hundred years ago.

Further along is the very attractive 17th century Old Hall, a long, low, gabled building that could have been lifted straight out of a Cotswold village. It's mellow stone walls are clad in wisteria, but it's also the scene of our next ghostly encounter.

Youlgreave Old Hall, the scene of a ghostly encounter

The skirmishes that took place between the Cavaliers and Roundheads during the Civil War have certainly left their mark, not only on our history but on our psychic landscape. Ghosts in the distinctive uniform of each side turn up quite regularly – although sadly not around Fulwood's Castle in Middleton, the earlier section of our walk. Just over a mile away, the occupants of Youlgreave Hall wait in trepidation for November when they are likely to be woken by the sound of ghostly swords clashing in one of the bedrooms.

It is now referred to as the Duel Room as this is where two Civil War soldiers, a Cavalier and a Roundhead are reputed to have fought to the death one dark November night back in the 1640s. The fight is said to be re-enact on each anniversary.

Many years ago, technicians were called in to make a recording of this conflict. The clash of swords and the 17th century cries and curses of the men would surely make great listening. Everything was set. The commentator sat waiting, the sound recordists held their breath in anticipation and sure enough the sounds began to materialise in the best ghost story tradition, then they ceased. The commentator dashed over to where the sound recordists crouched over their equipment. Did you hear it? Did you get it alright?'he asked excitedly.

Cause I didnt,' snapped the engineer. you switched off the microphone.'

The commentator denied it and went to check. Sure enough not only had the microphone been switched off, the electricity had also been disconnected. They had checked and double checked before they left it and everyone present denied touching it, so what had happened, who had stopped the recording?

After a short distance, the narrow street opens up into Fountain Square and in the centre, is the circular water storage tank known as the Fountain built in 1829 to provide drinking water for the villagers, piped from a spring near Mawstone Mine. During the week of June 24[th,] well dressing takes place here at the fountain and five other old well sites throughout the village.

To your left is the Post Office and across the road on your right is the old Co-op building, now the Youth Hostel. Its three storey Victorian façade stands tall and gaunt and its windows are still decorated with the characteristic lettering of the Co-operative Society which occupied the building until 1968. The building had its fleeting moment of fame when it appeared as a fictional store in the film of D.H Lawrence's novel *The Virgin and The Gypsy*. Youlgreave featured as Congreave.

A more famous building on the edge of the square is Thimble Cottage which according to the Guinness Book of Records, August 9th 2000, is the smallest detached house in the world. It's a tiny one up, one down cottage with a ladder for a staircase. Its miniscule dimensions are a mere 11ft 10inches x10ft 3 inches x 12ft 2 inches high and it's grade II listed. It has been a butcher's shop, a cobblers, an antique shop and about 100 years ago, housed a family of eight although it was last used as a home in the early 1930s. After lying empty for many years, it is now undergoing a sympathetic restoration.

Leaving Fountain Square, over to your right is the Bull's Head, an attractive old coaching inn with a coaching arch decorated with a carved bull's head. In the 19th century, Jane Shimwell, the youngest daughter of the landlord married Alexander MacDougal, the inventor of self-raising flour. She became Lady MacDougal when he became knighted. Further along amongst the old cottages is a clutch of traditional shops.

'There were twenty seven shops in the village in my youth,' recalled one old timer who had lived in Youlgreave all his life.' Nowadays we have just two butchers, a general store, and a post office.'

Mrs Johnson, a former Youlgreave resident had the gift of prediction although she would probably never have foreseen the demise of the village shops. She accredited her special gift to the fact that she was a twin born at midnight. It was said that she was able to foretell the name, or at least the initials of the girl a young man was destined to marry. To do this, Mrs Johnson would place a large iron key ring on the young man's forefinger. He would then be given a bible and told to read a specific verse after which he would recite the letters of the alphabet. When he reached certain letters spelling out her name or initials, the key ring would begin to revolve rapidly round his finger.

Continue until reaching the church. Go through the gate and walk round the right of the church to reach the south door. Standing in the churchyard opposite this door are the steps of the old village cross moved here from Fountain Square when the Fountain was installed. An upturned font is placed on the stone base, but sadly the sun-dial that sat on top is now missing.

The steps of the old village cross, now in the churchyard

The parish church of All Saints', Youlgreave is one of the oldest and largest mediæval churches in the Peak District and reflects the wider history of the parish which in mediaeval times was huge. As well as Youlgreave, it included the townships of Middleton, Smerrill, Birchover, Gratton and Stanton, the villages of Alport and Conksbury and the chapelries of Winster and Elton. Parishioners from all these far flung places were buried at Youlgreave, but only the wealthy made their final journey on a horse drawn hearse. The majority were borne on the shoulders of relatives and friends along the nearest routes which became known as Coffin Ways. This usually meant that coffins had to be carried for miles, so villagers put chairs outside their houses for the bearers to take a break.

All Saints' Church is well worth a visit, but our interest lies in the oldest monument in the church. To the left of the altar lies the tomb of Sir John Rossington, dating from the early 14th century.

The stone effigy of Sir John Rossington whose heart leapt into his hands when a trapped hare metamorphasised into a beautiful woman

The stone effigy of Sir John Rossington lies cross-legged, dressed in a quilted gambeson, his head on a pillow, his feet on a dog and holding a heart in his hands. According to the story behind this, Sir John cornered a hare that ran into the church for sanctuary and finding itself trapped, suddenly turned into a beautiful woman. Sir John was so shocked that his heart leapt into his hands where it still rests.

The legends of many cultures refer to deities changing into animal or human form, and we are weaned on folk-tales in which people are metamorphosised into lowly animals; Beauty and the Beast, and the Princess and the Frog spring to mind. But this shape shifting or changing was not just a thing of fairy tales. People actually believed that witches were not only able to transform people, but were able to transform themselves into whatever bird or animal they desired. For speed, the hare was a favourite shape adopted by witches and if a hunter wounded a hare and later saw a village woman wounded in the same part of the body, this was considered proof that she had changed shape and was therefore a witch. Similar tales tell of hunters killing hares that metamorphosed back into human corpses, so the story of Sir John Rossington is not unique, and itš not new. Itš been told around this ancient settlement for seven centuries.

Opposite the church is the George Hotel although it might be more correct to call it the Four George's as it seems to be undecided as to which King George it's honouring. The inn sign and the wine list gives documentation to four, spanning a period from George I (1714-27) to George IV (1820-30). If you need an escape route, you can catch the bus back to Alport from outside the George Hotel.

To continue our walk, we must leave the churchyard by the same gate we entered and turn immediately left into Bradford Road, leading to Mawstone Lane. Follow this lane steeply down then just before the last house on the left, Braemar House, bear off to the left along an enclosed path passing behind Braemar House down to meet a packhorse bridge across the River Bradford. Cross the bridge – 6 – and follow the wide gravel track to the left heading down through the valley. The River Bradford is to your left. Where this track bends up to the right, go straight on through a kissing gate then follow the path through a field to soon rejoin the river again.

Follow the path of the river downstream passing the limestone outcrop of Rhienstor, a popular climbing spot. When you reach a gate across the track on the outskirts of Alport, head through the gate, over the river bridge – 7 – and back to where you have parked your car.

4: A Gruesome Inn, Haunted Station, Ghosts, Boggarts and Brooding Ruins

ROWSLEY – DARLEY DALE – MATLOCK
Distance 6¾ Miles (10·90km) with return by train from Matlock Riverside to Rowsley South, or 10½ Miles (17km) overall

This is a wonderful walk with seven ghostly tales. It stretches from Rowsley following the River Derwent through to Matlock. There are

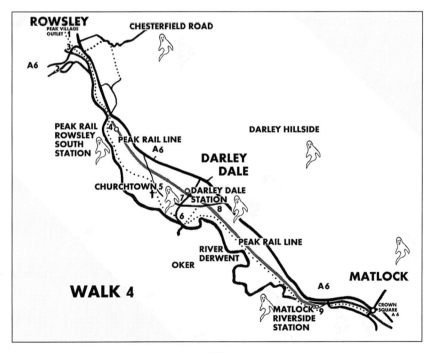

suggestions for breaking your journey to visit the oldest yew tree in Britain, a working Carriage Museum, and a haunted railway station. It's also a must for train buffs and those who love nostalgia as we recommend that your return journey is taken on the old steam train that travels along this valley on Sundays from April to September. It will add an extra spine-chilling factor to your walk as this railway is definitely haunted You can dine in the Palatine restaurant car which seats up to 71 people or participate in one of the special events whether it's a Santa and Steam special, a Warring Forties re-enactment of life in the war years, or the Halloween Ghost Train which guarantees to get your spine tingling. Contact Peak Rail on 01629 580381 to find out more details and times.

To reach Rowsley, take the A6 south from Bakewell. Enter Rowsley and after a few hundred yards take the B6012 Chatsworth Road on your left. Turn left between the houses to the well signed Peak Village Outlet Shopping Centre – 1 – and follow the road round into the car park.

Rowsley is a village divided by the River Derwent spanned by a 15th century bridge. To the west of the river is Great Rowsley, the original settlement with its stone cottages, water fountain and St Katherine's Church. At the centre is The Peacock Hotel built in 1652 as a yeoman's house. For a period it was used as the Dower House of Haddon Hall who held the manor of Rowsley, but has been an inn since the 1820s. The name reflects the family coat of arms which features a peacock. When I asked if the Peacock Hotel was haunted, I was told – 'We don't do ghosts!'

The settlement on the eastern side of the river was once known as Little Rowsley and was developed following the arrival in 1849 of the Midland Railway Line linking London St Pancras with Manchester Central. Or at least that was supposed to be the final destination, but the line terminated at Rowsley station, designed by Joseph Paxton of Crystal Palace fame, because the Duke of Devonshire would not allow the railway line to cross Chatsworth Park. In that first year, 80,000 people alighted at Rowsley station and walked the 1½ mile route to visit Chatsworth.

It wasn't until 1863 that an alternative route could be cut through the Wye Valley across the Duke of Rutland's estate, although when passing Haddon Hall, it was concealed from view in deep cuttings and tunnels. To serve this modified route, a new station called Rowsley South was built a mile down the track, leaving Paxton's station demoted and marooned. One hundred years later – 1968, the stretch of railway between Matlock and Buxton was axed in Beeching's reforms and has since been put to other uses. From Bakewell north it becomes

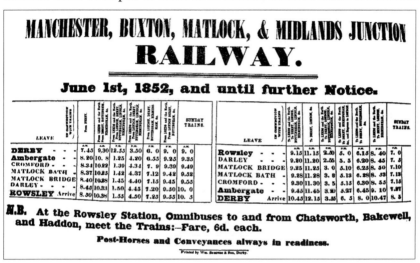

The timetable of the Midland Mainline train from London St Pancras which terminated at Rowsley. Note the fare of 6d for the use of omnibuses to and from Chatsworth, Bakewell and Haddon

Matlock Station is now the last stop on the line

the Monsal Trail for walkers, from Rowsley South to Matlock Riverside, it has been re-developed by Peak Rail bringing steam trains back to the valley.

THE WALK

Before setting off on our walk, take a look at the Rowsley station designed by Paxton. It had stood for years in the old railway yard, but when that was redeveloped as the Peak Village Shopping Centre, Paxton's railway station took on a new lease of life as a retail outlet and centre-piece.

Paxton's station was marooned when the railway line continued from Rowsley

Leave the shopping centre and with your back to the buildings, turn left to take the footpath in front of the Grouse and Claret Public House into Great Rowsley. While here, we highly recommend a visit to Caudwell's Mill and Craft Centre – 2 – Derbyshire's unique, grade II listed flour mill, and the only complete Victorian water turbine-powered roller mill in the country, power-driven by water from the River Wye. A mill has stood on this site for at least 400 years. The present mill built in 1874 by John Caudwell, was run as a family business for over a century and now fully restored is one of the last of its kind operating in the country. It uses the same process as the giant modern mills which provide most of the flour for our bread today, but at Caudwell's Mill, it is at a speed and on a scale that takes us back a hundred years. You are able to see four floors of fascinating, automatic machinery, most of which is still driven by belts, often leather, and pulleys from line shafts. Elevators and Archimedean screws abound. The mill is powered by two water turbines, the larger installed in 1914 to drive the flour mill and the smaller installed in 1898, for the provender mill and which, today, also generates the electricity used in the mill. Caudwell's historic mill is open daily for flour sales with a choice of over 20 specialist flours.

To reach the mill, cross the A6, turn right, cross the bridge over the River Derwent, then take the second left into the yard of Caudwell's Mill.

To continue our walk, return to the A6, retrace your steps over the bridge then after 100 yards turn right into Old Station Close – 3. Proceed past the car park on your right and walk as far as you can until a gap on the right leads you into the trees. Here is the confluence of the rivers Derwent and Wye which from this point become the River Derwent.

After approximately ¾ mile you will reach Nanny Goat Crossing and the edge of the Peak Rail site – 4. This tranquil setting is the present terminus of the railway line at Rowsley South Station. It was previously the 28 acre site of the ex-LMS/British Railways locomotive depot. Now there are 200 free parking spaces, a converted coach shop, a newly built gift shop, ticket office and toilet facilities. If as we suggest, you return by train, this is where the line terminates. It's also haunted.

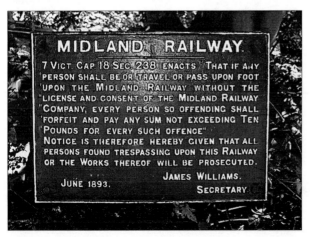

The old warning sign at Rowsley South Station

'A national group of paranormal experts are trying to prove whether or not Rowsley station is haunted', according to a report in the *Matlock Mercury*. After his visit, Jack Phillips, vice president of the Society for Paranormal Research is reported as saying; This is absolutely fantastic. Suffice to say there was enough going on for us to arrange to go back. It's the strangest place I have ever been to in 20 years of paranormal investigation.'

The group managed to gain photographic evidence of strange phenomena and audio recordings of voices answering questions. In addition, Mr Phillips claims the group heard the sound of a steam train thundering along track that has not been used for years.

Mr Phillips added; 'As a parapsychologist, I am satisfied that Rowsley train station is paranormally active. It is definitely worthy of further investigation.'

From Peak Rail Rowsley South, bear right at the side of the river, then on entering the first field follow the hedge on your left, not the river. This is part of the Derwent Valley Heritage Way which runs almost the full length of the River Derwent from the Ladybower reservoir in the north to the Derwent Mouth, south of Derby.

As you walk along this route, look again over to the hillside on your left which is the setting for our next ghost story.

On the night of the first full moon in March, echoes of a 400 year old tragedy resound above Darley Hillside as a phantom horseman sets off on a desperate search for his wife and family.

A phantom horseman can be seen on the first night of the full moon in March

Back in the 17th century, Henry Columbell, his wife Jane and their two young children were returning to the Columbell ancestral home at Darley Nether Hall after their annual seasonal visit to Eckington where they had been staying at Jane's father's home.

Escorted by only three servants, the little cavalcade was faced with mile after mile of stony, muddy tracks, and the going was especially slow as Jane was in the latter stages of pregnancy and being carried in a horse litter. Henry rode beside the litter, and their two small children were being carried in the arms of menservants.

As the day wore on, sleet began to fall and the skies turned dark, but the small group eventually reached the Chesterfield home of a relative where they spent the night.

The next day the party made steady progress as they began their arduous climb towards Wadshelf and the open moors above Holymoorside. All around them stretched an endless expanse of open moorland with no shelter against the biting winds that blew across the desolate waste land. It was a cold, tiring journey but worse was to come because dark storm clouds were gathering in the distance. Bad weather was approaching and they were in the middle of no-where. To return to their Chesterfield kin would take almost as long as to go on but they would soon be in dire need of help. Henry knew that if he rode fast he could reach Darley Nether Hall and return with more men and provisions before nightfall, so taking just one man-servant, he set off at a desperate gallop, leaving his family with two menservants to struggle on.

The snowstorm broke before Henry Columbell even reached Darley Nether Hall, sweeping in on a furious blizzard that showed no sign of abating. Henry's attempts to return for his family brought the horses to the ground and for three long days every attempt at rescue was thwarted by the blizzard that raged day and night. Finally they were able to set off battling against huge snow-drifts but to no avail. They searched in vain and Henry was utterly distraught when his beloved wife and children were eventually found huddled together in a hollow in the middle of the exposed moors.

The tragedy broke his heart and stole his reason. From then on until his death four years later, he would gallop over the moors on moonlit nights calling his wife's name in his desperate search, and his ghost continues to do exactly the same.

If you should be on the bleak, open moorlands round Farley and Darley hillside on the first night of the full moon in March, you might even encounter the ghost of Henry Columbell as he gallops by in his fruitless search.

Continue through the next field to the left of a short stretch of hedge ahead. In the third field, head for the stile beside the gate across on the other side of the field. In the fourth field, aim to the right of the stone barn ahead. Beyond that, walk along the left side of the fifth field. There's an interesting stone step-stile at the end of this field. Walk along the track beyond, ignoring all turns to left and right until you reach a tarmac access road which brings you to Churchtown – 5. At the T junction with Church Lane, turn right.

This is also known as Ghost Lane because apparently during the 17th century, a Scottish peddler was robbed and murdered here. Ever since, his ghost is said to haunt the area between the large sycamore tree and the churchyard of St Helen's church.

St Helen's Church on Church Lane which is also known as Ghost Lane

On your right is St Helen's church where the Columbell family coat of arms can still be seen on a plaque inside the Columbell Quire where the bodies of Henry Columbell, his wife Jane and their two young children were laid to rest. This is one of the only reminders we have of the previous tale, as Darley Nether Hall fell into ruins and was eventually pulled down in 1776. Now in its place we have streets with names like Old Hall Close, Hall Rise, Hall Dale View and Columbell Way.

Most people visit the churchyard to see what is believed to be one of, if not the oldest tree in England, the Darley Yew. It is estimated to be 2,000 years old, is just over 30ft in circumference and is actually marked on ordnance survey maps.

Leave the churchyard and turn right, then after a short distance, take the footpath on your right cutting diagonally across the first field, crossing the stream and heading south down the next field to meet the stream again on your left. Follow it through with the River Derwent on your right to a T junction with the B5057, Station Road leading from Darley Dale to Wensley and Winster. This area is called Darley Bridge – 6.

To visit Darley Dale Railway station – 7, the central station on this short stretch of line, turn left and walk up Station Road until reaching the gated level crossing.

Here you can enjoy a nostalgic trip into the railways past with a visit to the shop and exhibition which depicts the history of rebuilding the line by devoted volunteers over the last sixteen years. You might also have a ghostly experience.

Darley Dale Station is haunted by a woman and a fireman

A ghostly fireman is said to haunt the sheds at Darley Dale station and another ghost is said to be a young woman.

Jackie Statham, managing director for Peak Rail said; In Darley Dale there has always been the story of a woman who committed suicide on the railway line. I've looked into some records but I've not found any evidence of this yet, but the ghost of a young woman is certainly said to haunt the tracks.'

One of the society members stayed for a time in a camper van on the site and on several occasions he was convinced he had experienced paranormal activity.

After reports of a number of ghostly sightings, it was decided to invite The Society for Paranormal Research to visit Darley Dale station, and in 2008, they timed their visit to coincide with the Warring Forties weekend. These weekends are held annually and are very popular. They re-create the atmosphere of the 1940s, and to get you in the mood, there are wartime, military and vintage vehicle displays, troop and evacuee trains, wartime memorabilia, Home Front and WVS kitchen displays, together with live music, jive and jitterbug demonstrations and tea dances. Re-enactors and visitors alike don period clothing to authenticate the scene.

Jackie added; We have the 1940s weekend every year and last year members of the paranormal group saw a soldier walking down the track. It had gone midnight and they thought it was a person in costume, but when they got closer, he just vanished.'

The group used a professional medium to help with their investigation and Jack Phillips, vice president of the society believes the nostalgia weekend was a good opportunity for a time-slip. He said, A time slip is when everything goes blurred and you're transported back in time for a few seconds. It's you who appears as a ghost in another time.'

The annual Halloween night celebration is the time for relating a few ghostly stories and as this is usually attended by children, the tales are deliberately kept light. One of the volunteers was telling a group of children how when the railway closed no one bothered to tell the signalman who worked the signals from his box high above the line. There he stayed in solitary confinement until his death and now his ghost is still there. She gestured to the signal box standing beside the line and the group went hysterical. A colleague had borrowed a skeleton and lit it with a weird blue light for added effect.

On my recent visit to Darley Dale station, I was wondering round the exhibits in the station building. I was alone apart from a large dog that was fast asleep on a dog bed in the corner of the room. Although I would have liked to take a look at the photographs on the wall behind the dog, I decided it was probably advisable not to disturb him. I was just about to turn away when the dog suddenly let out a pitiful howl and leapt up as though struck by a sudden unexpected pain. The dog then stood glaring at something behind me and he didnt look too friendly or comfortable. I half turned but there was nothing there and it wasnt until later that the thought crossed my mind that the dogs pain may have been inflicted by a kick from an invisible foot. Dogs are extremely sensitive to spirit and the dogs reaction was exactly what you would expect if a spirit presence was nearby.

The train just leaving Darley Dale Station

Is the signal box really haunted?

The driver and his mate waiting until it's time to leave the station

While in this area, a visit to Redhouse Stables and Working Carriage Museum is also recommended. From Darley Bridge proceed up Station Road but before reaching Darley Dale Station take the Old Road to your right. Here at the museum you can see one of the finest collections of original horse drawn vehicles and equipment in Britain. These are the magnificent coaches and carriages that appear in so many historical dramas in films and TV. One of the most unusual aspects of the collection is that it is a working museum and the vehicles and horses are regularly out on the roads being used. It is possible to hire one of these magnificent vehicles or join one of the regular trips through the delightful Derbyshire countryside, so for details telephone 01629 733583. A coach from Redhouse stables features in Walk 7.

To continue our walk, return to Darley Bridge – 6, and just past the Square and Compass pub before the road bears right over the bridge, take the second of two squeeze stiles on your left. Walk along the track immediately to the left of the farm buildings, Flatts Farm. At the end of the track pass through another squeeze stile and walk beside the wall on your left. Stay beside the wall in the second field. Walk across the middle of the third field and as you enter a fourth field, turn left immediately to cross a bridge over Warney Brook. This feeds into the River Derwent which is on your right. Follow the path up to the railway line and turn right with the railway line on your left – 8.

Look over to your right where you will see a tree on a solitary peak known as Oker Hill. In 1838 this inspired Wordsworth to write The Keepsake, a sonnet which relates to a legend about two brothers who each planted a sycamore tree on the summit of the hill before parting for ever. One brother made a success of his life and the tree flourished, the other brother was a failure and his tree withered and died.

You are now passing the disused Cawdor Quarry site on your right. Quarries abound within the Peak District and there is a close correlation between them and the lights, humming noises and other paranormal phenomena reported in many areas. Many believe that anything that disturbs the ground also releases the wrath of the spirits and kicks earth energy into life. That would appear to be the case at Cawdor Quarry.

70

The old buildings on Cawdor Quarry were definitely haunted

An early proposal to develop the disused Cawdor Quarry site at Matlock resulted in members of the public being asked to air their views. Some did it in writing and the most unexpected letter of protest, although unsigned, came from someone who stated that the development would never go ahead because the Standbark Boggart would not allow it. Bearing in mind that this multi-million pound development scheme was the biggest ever considered in the area, the councillors of the Derbyshire Dales District were treading very carefully, but even so, such a letter was dismissed as superstitious mumbo jumbo. Planning officer Roger Yarwood made the comment I think we would have trouble sustaining a planning appeal on the basis of disturbing a ghost.'

Tarmac tried and failed to acquire the necessary permission and in 1994 the site was sold to the Hughes organization. The immense cost of installing the necessary relief road was partly met by Sainsbury's who in 1998 bought ten acres of the site to build a supermarket, but at every stage there was opposition and many delays which meant that the price of developing the remainder of the site was escalating out of control.

But to go back to that initial letter and the Standbark Boggart! Strange things had begun happening at Cawdor Commercials who manufactured truck bodies in one of the large buildings on the quarry site. These men were tough no-nonsense guys who didnt believe in ghosts, or at least they hadnt until things got so bad they could find no other explanation. In the office corridor, people heard sounds which corresponded exactly with the measured tread of human footsteps. They stopped as they reached the door. No-one ever appeared, and going to check, the corridor was always empty. Cold draughts were often felt in the corridor and one member of the office staff was trapped in the toilet by an unseen, though felt presence. Another regular sound was the banging on the sides of the building which were made of corrugated sheeting. Again, when going to check, no-one was ever there and it was impossible for any troublesome person playing a prank to have got away without being seen.

There was always the sense of being watched, and followed. People were touched, machinery malfunctioned and the overhead crane mysteriously moved. The forks of the fork-lift truck fell down nearly scaring the guys to death. Firstly, from a safety point of view it was never left with the forks in the air, but on this occasion it was, despite no-one having done it. As one of the guys said, It wasnt just the fact that no one was near it, or the fact that the forks should not have been up, it was the way it fell as if someone was watching our reaction and deliberately paused it mid-fall to get the maximum response. It was lever operated and just too spooky for it to be an accidental fall.'Prior to this the company operated a night shift, but from then on the guys were too scared and all refused to work at night. It wasnt long after this that they moved out and re-sited the company away from the area.

The Cawdor Quarry development has been a Stop/Start operation right from the very start. The cost of development has escalated; two lots of owners have gone bankrupt and still there is nothing happening on the site. If the Standbark Boggart is responsible for all this confusion and chaos he's certainly a powerful force to reckon with.

Continue along beside the railway line for 1¼ miles until reaching Matlock Riverside Station – 9. There are plans to take this line into Matlock station when the next stage of the building work takes place, but at the moment, this is the end of the line.

At the moment, this is the end of the line for Peak Rail

*The newly resurfaced riverside path
continues into Matlock*

*A nostalgic railway poster
advertising Matlock as the
Switzerland of England
and metropolis
of hydropathy*

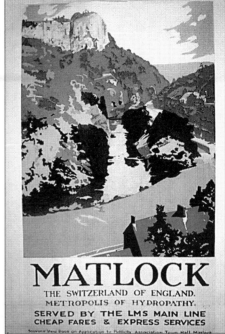

MATLOCK

THE SWITZERLAND OF ENGLAND.
METROPOLIS OF HYDROPATHY.
SERVED BY THE LMS MAIN LINE
CHEAP FARES & EXPRESS SERVICES

At the moment to visit Matlock – 10, from Matlock Riverside Station, continue along the riverside path, passing under the newly constructed A6. It's a ten minute walk to Matlock along a surfaced path which comes out next to the old road bridge over the Derwent in the centre of the town.

This area expanded significantly in the mid 1800s because of a local hosiery manufacturer named John Smedley who became involved in the hydropathic and medicinal qualities of Matlock's water. Spa towns such as Buxton had long utilised their thermal springs for internal consumption and bathing, but in the mid 1800's John Smedley introduced hydrotherapy which offered nearly 300 different water treatments. The face of Matlock was changed forever as huge numbers of infirm visitor flocked to the area and at least 26 hydros opened up in Matlock alone.

John Smedley's main hydro/hotel was the very impressive building that is now the County Offices half way up Bank Road, one of the steepest streets in the area, but thanks to the financial backing of Sir George Newnes, a native of Matlock, on March 26th 1893, the Matlock Steep Gradient Tramway was launched. It covered a distance of five eighths of a mile, had a speed of 5½ miles per hour and climbed a 1 in 5.5 gradient, making it, at the time, the world's steepest tramway system. It operated for almost 35 years, closing on September 30th 1927. The tram shelter in Crown Square is now in Hall Leys Park, and the lettered glass window is on display at Crich Transport Village, five miles south of Matlock

Matlock in the early 20th century.
Looking over the bridge up Bank Road.
Smedley's Hydro is the long building on
the left near the skyline

Crown Square looking over the bridge
in the opposite direction.
The tramway terminus, now in
Hall Leys Park, is on the right

The home John Smedley built for himself between 1862-8 at a cost of £60,000 was called Riber Castle but now its no more than a brooding ruin that dominates the Matlock skyline from its 853ft high perch. Because of its remote and inaccessible position, the castle had its own well and gas-producing plant for lighting the lavish interior. When John Smedley died in 1874, his widow Caroline continued to live there, then the building was sold in 1888 and became a boys school until 1929. It was never to be lived in again and fell into gradual decline. The Matlock Urban Council purchased it for £1,150 and for a time it was used as a store for the War Office, but it was later left to become a ruined shell.

In 1962, it was purchased by a group of zoologists for £540 and until the end of the 20th century the buildings and surrounding area were used as a zoo. In recent years a move has been made to revamp the site and build new housing on what has become known as Smedley's Folly, but will the spectres that haunt the site approve?

The most prolific ghost is said to be a lady in blue who patrols the grounds and wonders through the empty corridors and rooms. One woman who saw her while walking her dogs described her as having untidy hair, a gentle expression and sad, shadowed eyes. Could this be Caroline Smedley who, although given little recognition, took an active part in the hydropathic establishment alongside her husband.

At times people have also seen a figure in military uniform who not only marches round the walls, but through them too. He was witnessed by Mr & Mrs Linnett in 1973. Like many people who have had similar experiences, seeing him so fleetingly made them question whether he was there at all, or just a trick of the light?

*Riber Castle
is now no more
than a brooding ruin*

For your return journey you can either retrace your steps or we suggest you take a journey back in time on a steam train along its complete 4 mile route from Matlock Riverside Station back to Rowsley South.

Resuming our walk at the Peak Rail site at Rowsley South – 4 – leave by the entrance onto the A6. Turn left, cross at the pelican crossing and proceed up Northwood Lane. After 200 yards as the road does a sharp right turn uphill, turn left – 11. Continue for about 300 yards. Bear right uphill and eventually you reach Tinkersley Farm. Take the step-over stile beside the gate and keep forward with the property to your right. Cross a stile and walk through the field beyond with the farmhouse above you on the right. The level path brings you to Copy Wood.

Proceed along the obvious path through the wood – 12. Some 500 yards later you emerge into a small, private golf course. Walk across this, keeping on the same level, to reach a step-over stile beside a farm gate. This brings you onto the road which runs from Rowsley up over some of the most desolate moorland in the area, and passes a few yards away from an isolated property called The Woodlands which is the setting for our final ghost story on this walk.

The Woodlands is a secluded property with a history of mysterious fires which legend tells us can be traced back to centuries ago, when the site was occupied by a lonely wayside inn named The Quiet Woman.' But the landlady was not just quiet, she was surly and sullen and her unpleasant attitude discouraged customers who stopped for sustenance and shelter. Some tales tell that not only did she discourage them, she made a habit of robbing and murdering them, then buried their bodies in the cellar.

Understandably, business became so bad that the landlord had to find some other form of employment, and turned to highway robbery to supplement their income. Then one dark night, this robber/landlord was wounded by his intended victim, who broke free and headed for the supposed safety of the inn.

A few minutes later, his injured assailant arrived home and was pushed into the cellar to hide. In the scuffled that ensued, an oil lamp was knocked over and fire spread rapidly across the room, trapping the unfortunate man in the cellar. The landlady escaped the fire but the experience left her deranged. Another version said she was hanged for her crimes, but returned to re-enact the accident for eternity.

The vastly altered building became a farm-house then in 1966, a country club known as Moor Lane Sporting Club on the site was gutted by fire. The owner confided to friends that he had experienced odd happenings and was especially concerned that his dog took fright for no apparent reason. He probably had reason to worry because during subsequent re-building, a caravan he occupied was also gutted by fire. Now private property The Woodlands gives no hint of its gruesome past

To complete the final stages of our walk, turn left downhill passing Toll Bar Cottage, then turn left down the path – 13 – on the far side of the driveway leading to Woodside. Follow this path beside a hedge on your left to enter a field. Keep down the right side of this, then the obvious path to reach the A6 – 14. Cross with care and continue straight forward along the A6, turn right along the footpath in front of the Grouse and Claret which brings you to the car park which is the start/end of this walk.

5: Malevolent Spirits, Nine Naughty Ladies, A Votive Tree and Domestic Disturbances

BIRCHOVER GHOST WALK
Distance 3⅛ Miles (5km)

Birchover is an ancient village in the middle of magnificent rock scenery six miles south-east of Bakewell. It is mentioned in the Domesday Book, but the area is rich with evidence of primitive man's

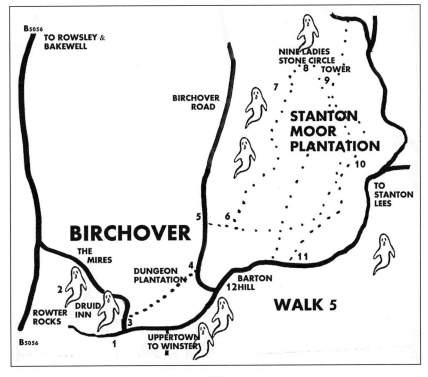

passage, and has the reputation of being a former stronghold of pagan worship. During the early 20th century, father and son team J.C. and J.P Heathcote of Birchover excavated many of the burial mounds on Stanton Moor where the Bronze Age people buried the ashes of their dead in urns. The Heathcotes displayed their finds in a small museum they set up at the village Post Office. Sadly the museum and post office have since gone, and the relics have been moved to the Sheffield Weston Park Museum.

To reach Birchover from Bakewell, take the A6 south and just after passing Haddon Hall, take the B5056 on your right. The road initially runs beside the River Lathkill. After about 2·3 miles (3·70km) turn left along a minor road to Birchover. As you enter the village the road make a sharp left turn. The Druid Inn is on your right. Park on the road in Birchover in the vicinity of the Druid Inn, or in The Druid Inn car park if you intend to participate in the hospitality of the house.

THE WALK

Leave the car park – 1, cross the lane and facing the Druid Inn, bear left through a gap in the wall which gives access to Rowter rocks – 2, the impressive pile of gritstone megaliths that stand just behind the inn. This can be visited at the beginning or end of your walk, but we prefer it at the beginning.

The impressive Rowter Rocks are believed to be the site of a Druid temple, but date back to pre-history, and are the haunt of many malevolent spirits

78

The fame of Rowter rocks probably resulted from the work of a much quoted early antiquarian archaeologist, the celebrated Druid, Rev. Dr. William Stukeley (1687-1765). He is responsible for linking the Druids with stone circles and famously claimed Stonehenge was built by them as a Druid Temple, a place of worship and sacrifice. Stukeley also ascribed the same to various Derbyshire sites including Arbor Low, Stanton Moor and Rowter Rocks, but scientific advances in carbon-dating has since shown that he was wrong. Most of these sites were in use two to three thousand years earlier.

The Druid Temple at Rowter Rocks may very well have been used by the Druids and definitely goes back into pre-history, but it was reputedly modelled by the Reverend Thomas Eyre of Rowter Hall between 1680-1710 as a sort of Druid Folly for his own use. He may have been a colleague of Rev. William Stukeley and was certainly influenced by him.

Formerly Rowter Rocks were known as Rooter Rocks, from roos meaning to rock, because the outcrop was famed for its rocking stones until 1799 when a gang of 14 youths deliberately dislodged a 50 ton rocking stone poised near the summit. Since then, a 12ft oval boulder which could be rocked with just a finger and thumb has also been immobilised, as have a pile of seven rocks formerly set in motion by pushing the one at the bottom.

These heaps of rocks may no longer rock but they form majestic mounds piled high, smoothed and weathered into abstract shapes that are immensely impressive. It helps to be as nimble as a mountain goat to climb up, through and round them, and beware of the steep drop barely disguised by the overgrown vegetation, and the chasms that seem to be bottomless. There are alcoves and caves that reach deep into the inner core, so it is advisable to take a torch to explore them.

Over to one side are a series of hewn steps that lead to a reasonably flat stone mass, but what singles this out for special attention is that it has an elongated notch hewn to form seating, complete with back support and arm rests that divide the seat into three, rather like seats in a cinema.

It may be fanciful to speculate that this was once the seat of the Arch-Druid, who ranked by his advisers, would sit and survey the topographical landscape stretched out in front of him, because Rowter rocks command the most amazing views (although now obstructed by vegetation). Sitting here surveying the scene, it is not difficult to see why an ancient site like this has long been regarded as a place of power where unusual forces can manifest. Folk memory, rumours and anecdotes from visitors have been augmented by the claims of psychics, so there is a wealth of evocative tales associated with Rowter Rocks.

Some say that Rowter Rocks are haunted by many malevolent spirits. A cloaked, ghostly figure is the most frequently seen, although on moonlit nights it is said that the whole area is filled with the sound of weeping and wailing. Could this be a throwback to a time when it was used for sacrificial purposes? Local legend says that if you sit in the afore mentioned middle arm-chair when the church clock has just struck midnight, you will hear the spirit of the wind whisper the name of your true love. Those with clairvoyant abilities might even see the tiny, winged, semi-translucent Sylphs as they dart past, particularly if they've first taken advantage of the hospitality of the Druid Inn, but due to the hazardous climbs and precipitous drops this is one place I'd never recommend anyone to visit at night without a couple of arc lights and an ambulance standing by.

After scrambling around Rowter Rocks, I was ready to partake of the hospitality of the Druid Inn.

The Druid Inn, where a ghostly spirit made her presence known

Although alleged to be of greater antiquity, the Druid Inn is actually of 18th century construction and probably resulted from the relative fame of an 1868 book by James Croston entitled *On Foot Through The Peak*. In this Croston quoted the celebrated Druid Rev. Dr William Stukeley and made reference to several supposed Druidic places in Derbyshire including Rowter Rocks. These claims had been echoed a generation later by fellow antiquarian archaeologists Dr Samuel Pegge, Major Rooke and Llewellyn Jewitt, who lived at Winster Hall featured in *Walk 6*.

Myths and legends were woven around these druidic places and early landlords of the Druid Inn sold tickets and acted as guides to visitors who came from all over the country to visit Rowter Rocks, a trade which continued until well into the 20th century.

Id heard that the Druid Inn was haunted by a kindly old lady with a warm caring smile, who sits in the corner of one of the downstairs rooms. My intuition led us to sit in the small room to the right of the front door. Was this the room where people have experienced her presence?

When the waiter brought our food I asked him about this, but he seemed unable to give me an answer. My enquiries seemed to be going nowhere when a magazine that had been on a unit in the corner of the room suddenly fell on the floor. There was no draught and no-one near, so it was strange that just one of the many books and magazines there should have fallen. As the waiter picked it up I recognised the magazine as one which I occasionally write for. I laughed as I pointed this out but as I took it from him to verify the statement, it fell open at one of my articles. I stared in disbelief. This was more than a coincidence. What were the odds against that kind of thing happening? I strongly believe that the little old lady was aware of my presence and decided to show me.

Leave the Druid Inn and turn left onto the main road – 3. After a short distance you will pass Mires trough, the original spring that supplied water to Birchover. In 2003, it was repaired and restored and now makes a pleasing roadside feature.

Just past the trough is a flight of rough stone steps and a signposted path which ascends steeply up the wooded hillside. Follow it for 600 yards until it reaches open ground and Birchover Road – 4. Turn left towards Stanton in the Peak and walk 400 yards ignoring a minor

The recently restored mires trough   *The footpath leads up through trees*

unmarked track off to the right. Shortly after on the brow of the hill, turn right up a sign posted footpath – 5. In 30 yards cross a stile onto Stanton Moor. Continue along a stony path with a fence on the right.

In the Bronze Age period, this area would have been covered with rich farm land and woodland, not the dry, peaty moors of today. Farming communities would have been dotted all around the area, and intermingled with the round houses where extended families would live together, would have been the burial mounds. More than 70 Bronze Age tumuli or burial mounds have been found dotted around on the 150 acre summit of Stanton Moor, recognisable as low hummocks in the heather.

People regularly request that their ashes are scattered on Stanton Moor, but it would appear that people were also buried on Stanton Moor as one example from the 1779 accounts of the Youlgreave Parish Constable states. '*At ye inquest of Bette Gregory, expenses of ye Jure (Jury) 8s.0d the Ale and bread and cheese to the men that went with the corpse 2s.0d. For ceredge of the Corpse on to Stanton More 2s6d. Pd to Stanton Officer for ye grave making and sum ale and eating 2s.0d'.*

Criss-crossing the moor are numerous hollowed out pathways that would have been eroded by the hooves of the lines of 30 or 40 pack-horses. These have now become the walks and recreational routes used by todays visitors who walk across the moor, to discover an area which is rich in stone circles, burial mounds and other remnants of our ancient past.

This is an area which is also rich in stories that include abduction by UFOs, reports of a spectral black dog, a ghostly monk, a headless horseman, a green man, a white lady and hovering lights. All these stories add to the atmosphere of the place.

Following the well trodden path, the first curiosity met along the way is the Cork stone – 6, a great upright stone with footholds and iron handholes, standing beside the footpath. Ascent it if you dare or can!

After 300 yards, turn left at a cross track signed to Nine Ladies Stone Circle. Head towards the open woodland ahead. After 500 yards, just before reaching the edge of the wood, deviate left for 50 yards along a clear path to an enclosure half hidden in the heather – 7. This enclosure is a ring cairn, a stone embankment built to surround a low burial mound or possibly the site of a funeral pyre, as many Bronze Age people were cremated in the open and their ashes scattered. Only certain important individuals were buried in tumuli, the stone lined chambers raised to form mounds. Grave goods have been found in these tumuli, but these were not rich pickings – mostly jars containing food and drink and a few simple arrow heads and tools for use in the afterlife.

Return to the path and the Nine Ladies stone circle – 8.

The Nine Ladies Stone Circle was once a sacred place where the milestones of a person's life would have been celebrated – religious ceremonies, rites of passage, rites connected with childbirth, puberty and marriage as well as death. The stone circle acted as a mystical wall, to contain the magic of the occasions while excluding everyday life.

Modern day witches with their respect for nature still meet on Stanton Moor and report a strong energy force in the area of the Nine Ladies Circle which is 35ft in diameter and surrounded by a shallow mound. To the south-west of the circle is the King stone or as some call it, the Fiddler's Chair. According to legend, the devil played his fiddle while nine ladies danced on the Sabbath, but God was so furious at their transgression that he turned them all into stone for disregarding his holy day. It's a story that is attached to many similar stone circles, but instead of being called ladies, they are called 'maidens' which is believed to be a corruption of 'meyn' meaning stone. This may be inchoate folk memory and over time has changed to ladies.

Whatever – there they still remain in their petrified state on this lonely moor, and when the wind blows across the hillside you can almost hear the screeching sound of a fiddle being played badly. A ghostly male figure dressed in black has often been seen standing just outside the circle. Could this be the devil or the fiddler or just a trick of the light?

The Nine Ladies stone circle was once a scared place
and can be very atmospheric

Another remnant from the past is the votive or rag tree on Stanton Moor, which is still used today. Rag trees are often hawthorns or trees that are associated with protection from the evil eye, and are believed to have special powers of healing They were seen and reported as early as the 4th century and were hung with strips of cloth which represent pleas for healing and improvement in fortune. One belief is that the tree itself bears the weight of the illnesses that people are trying to rid themselves of.

Festooned with rags, handkerchiefs, scarves and other items of clothing as well as garlands of flowers, by the time the offering rots off the branch, the request will apparently be granted.

Leaving the circle, turn right down a path to a stile. Cross the stile and turn right along a path with a fence on your right and a steep drop with excellent views to your left. After a few hundred yards you will pass the Reform Tower – 9 – on your right, built to commemorate the passing of Earl Grey's Reform Bill in 1832. This gave wider representation in government for the new up and coming middle classes and parliamentary democracy as we know it today.

Following the path south, continue along the Stanton Edge foot-path, soon passing a large boulder known as the Cat stone on your left – 10. This perimeter path gives some amazing sights over the Derwent valley with many far reaching views which are best appreciated on a fine day. In the 18th century, it was the custom of large land owners to entertain their guests by taking them on a tour of their estates in horse drawn carriages. Still known as the Duke's Drive, the scenic drive or ride along the edge of Stanton Moor which formed the boundary between the Stanton estate and the Haddon estate, with its panoramic views would have been a popular drive for the Duke of Rutland's London guests.

Stanton Moor Edge from where the views are quite spectacular

Descend with the path to a lane known as Barton Hill - 11, turn right and follow the road back to Birchover where this final selection of stories comes from. Because they relate to private houses that have since changed hands, we will deliberately not identify their precise locations

Many years ago, the secretary of Birchover WI told Clarence Daniel about several very peculiar incidents that happened at her aunts Birchover home.

She bought a picture of a horse and hung it over the fireplace but next morning the picture was propped up against the opposite wall, its cord unbroken, and glass intact. She re-hung it and the same thing happened again. After much deliberation, she hung it on the adjacent wall but again, next morning the picture was propped up against the opposite wall, its cord unbroken, and glass intact. She re-hung it, but the same thing happened again and again, until eventually she gave the picture away.

A year later another mysterious happening occurred at the same house. The eighteen year old daughter had begun collecting glass animals and birds which she displayed in a glass cabinet. Nothing strange occurred until she acquired a glass swan which she put in the glass cabinet with her other pieces, but it persistently refused to remain in its appointed position. At first she told herself that she was imagining it! That had to be the logical explanation, but when she found the swan reversed with its back on display she knew she wasnt. She considered the possibility of vibration that might have gradually moved the swan but as it didnt affect any of the other ornaments in the display, that was discounted. It would appear that this particular house has a rather choosy ghost that makes a habit of showing her displeasure at certain items, but I find the most bizarre story occurred when the ghost clearly didnt like the new wallpaper.

The lady of the house was papering the bedroom situated on the left side of the stairs, and the bedroom door which led onto the landing was open. She was standing on a step ladder attaching a length of wallpaper to the wall when suddenly something struck her in the middle of the back. Turning round, she looked down to see a light bulb on the floor, the only possible explanation for what had just hit her. The bulb was unbroken but what was most surprising was that it was the bulb from the hanging pendant light on the landing. By some means it had become detached and fallen, but instead of tumbling directly down the stairs, it had somehow defied the laws of gravity to swerve into the room and strike the decorator. When the bulb was replaced in the socket, it lit immediately so the delicate filament was surprisingly undamaged by its unusual journey.

A former vice-president of Holymoorside W.I. recounted to Clarence Daniel how, as a girl, she had stayed with a friend at Birchover in a house that had formerly been an inn. During the night, they were both woken by a noise and saw a light being carried along the passage outside their bedroom door. The previous night, her friends young brother had suffered from an attack of neuralgia and the girls assumed that it was he who had walked by on his way to obtain an aspirin. They called out to ask if he was alright but received no reply, so they got up to investigate and found him fast asleep in bed. No other members of the household had been awake until disturbed by the girls putting on the electric light, so who had walked along that corridor carrying what they had assumed was a torch, but could just as well have been a candle?

Another ghostly story that I am indebted to Clarence Daniel for concerns a gentleman called Dennis Slater and happened when he was a boy living in Birchover. Dennis and his brother had a terrifying experience as they lay in bed early one Sunday morning. Dawn was breaking, and in the dim light they saw a door open in a blank, papered wall. A man of large stature entered the room and stood resting his hands on the foot of the bed as he gazed at the fear-stricken occupants.

After standing for what seemed an interminably long time, the giant visitor left the room by the normal door and in the blank wall through which he had entered they found no sign of a crack or crevice in the wallpaper to identify the doorway through which the man had passed.

Continue to walk through the village – 12. To your left Uppertown Lane leads to Winster. If you wish to combine *Walks 5 & 6*, walk down Uppertown Lane until reaching the junction with the B5057. Turn left onto Elton Road which leads into the Main Street of Winster.

Continue the Birchover Walk through the village until reaching the Druid Inn at the far end, which is the start/end of this walk.

6: A Haunted Ore House, Phantom Footsteps, Ghost Lights and Flying Cats

WINSTER
Distance 2 Miles (3·25 km)

The old market town of Winster which first appeared in the Domesday Book as Winsterne, is situated in a valley and climbs irregularly up the side of a rocky eminence 6½ miles S.SE of Bakewell. In the centre is the restored Market Hall which dates from the late 17th - early 18th centuries. It is a reminder of when cheese markets and cattle fairs were

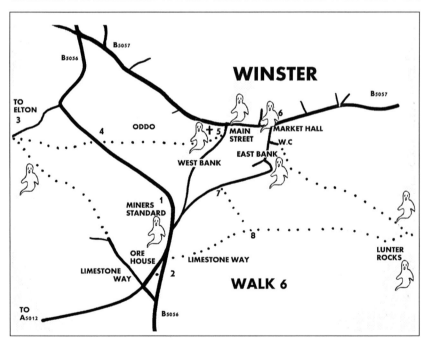

a prominent feature of local life, and has the distinction of being the first Peak District property acquired by the National Trust.

Winster is a village that is full of character and long held traditions like the Morris Dancing and the annual Pancake Race which are still celebrated along its period streets. It's the only village in Derbyshire to hold pancake races, a custom that goes back to the 15th century, and although it's not known exactly when the Winster pancake race started, it has a written history that goes back to 1870.

Winster was always an important lead mining town, so to reflect its lead mining heritage it seems fitting that we should begin our walk at The Miner's Standard – an old ale house named after the dish traditionally used by the miners for measuring the lead ore.

To reach Winster from Bakewell, take the A6 south passing through Rowsley and into Darley Dale. At the crossroads, turn right into Station Road, the B5057 to Wensley and Winster. Just down Station Road you will cross the railway line at the haunted Darley Dale Station featured in *Walk 4*. Continue along the B5057 for almost 3 miles (4.5km) to reach Winster. Pass through the village and just before the church turn left up West Bank. The Miners Standard is at the head of this lane where it meets the B5056

THE WALK

The Walk begins at the Miners Standard – 1 – a 17th century free house just outside the village. Built originally as a farmhouse by the Parker family in 1653, a tablet over the door shows the date and initials EP, EP and FP. Locals will tell you this stands for Every Person Entering Pays For a Pint, but in fact it's the initials of the original owners, a yeoman farmer named Edward Parker, his wife Elizabeth and son Francis. The hearth tax of 1670 gives Edward Parker as proprietor, payable for two hearths. The original building was quite substantial with four rooms on the ground floor, five on the second floor, 2 stables, one carriage shed, two piggeries, a brew house and a small place for sundries.

The mention of a brewhouse is interesting although it was not unusual for farms to brew ale and serve it to thirsty voyagers. Here, there would be no shortage of travellers because just at the rear of the building is the ancient Portway, one of the oldest of Derbyshire's trade routes – see also *Walk 3 & 10*. This would ensure a good passing trade which was boosted by the local lead mining community of Islington. From early days, the toxicity of lead was known to be a problem for both people and livestock, but it was widely believed that ale was an antidote to lead poisoning. It's therefore not surprising that the miners rejoiced in consuming plenty of medicinal ale and although it continued to be a working farm, it became known as the Miners Standard. This is the name of the wooden dish used by miners to measure lead ore.

A tablet over the door shows the date and initials of the origianl owners

The Miners Standard – reflects the area's lead mining tradition

Mill Close miners measuring lead ore using a wooden miners standard

With such a long and chequered history, it's not surprising to find that the Miners Standard has its fair share of ghosts. In 1839, John Smith, listed as a butter dealer lived here with his wife Mary and three young daughters Catherine, Dorothy and Emma. The sound of footsteps in an upper room draws attention to an unseen occupant who hums the first bars of the old nursery rhyme Three Blind Mice.' Customers who have caught the low quavering notes say that the voice is of a lady, as if soothing a small child to sleep.

Understandably this has attracted many paranormal groups who allege that the voice is that of Mary Smith singing to her little daughter Emma. They also claim to have made contact with a man who walks around upstairs. The name George has been mentioned and the current landlord can confirm that this was the name of his father–in–law who had the bedroom where the presence was detected. George's ashes are buried under the urn by the side of the car-park.

I believe you are haunted!' I said to the landlord. He laughed. It was obviously a question he was asked frequently.

We most certainly are,' he confirmed with a good humoured grin. But it doesnt bother us.'

To begin our walk, leave the Miners Standard, turn right and walk up the road. After a short distance the Elton and Newhaven road goes off to the right. We will walk along here, but first go to the flat topped, stone building just ahead. This is the best preserved Ore House in the Peak – 2. Years ago, local miners would have used this building like a modern night safe at a bank, but it was for the safe keeping of lead ore not money. It had a stone chute at the back where the newly extracted ore could be tipped at the end of a working day, and a vaulted ceiling

The Ore House –
the ancient equivalent of
our modern night safe

for security so that the ore could be kept temporarily under lock and key before being weighed. You can almost feel the presence of those long dead miners hanging around here in order to safeguard their claims.

Directly opposite the old Ore House is Mosey Mere. Water is very scarce in limestone areas like this because rain water seeps through the cracks in limestone. Mosey Mere only exists because a layer of volcanic rock under the surface of the ground holds the water. The mere supplied water to the mining settlement of Islington and was used by the packhorse trains on the old Portway. While the drovers took an overnight rest at the Miners Standard, the pack horses were watered at Mosey Mere beside which is an area of common ground where they were allowed to graze.

To return to our walk, leave the Ore House, return to the junction and turn left.

After a few minutes, turn right on reaching a stony side lane. This is the old Portway which was the major highway until the modern turn-pike road from Ashbourne to Haddon was built, and was known as Islington Lane. This is now part of the Limestone Way as you will see on the guide post which carries the ram's head motif of the Limestone Way. Although its ruins are now hardly discernable a once prosperous

lead mining settlement named Islington stood alongside this lane. Some historians refer to it as a lead miners shanty town, particularly as the industry went into decline in the late 18th century and many families had no other means of support. They had to enter the workhouse which was built directly opposite the common land we've just left.

Winster was once an important destination as this ancient stone stoop on Beeley Moor shows

This stretch of the old Portway is known as Islington Lane where the lost village of Islington has left the occasional ruin

The ram's head motif denotes the Limestone Way

Follow Islington Lane for about ½ mile ignoring Lickpenny Lane on the left.

Doreen Bullard has always known that she possessed a sixth sense because she was the seventh child of a seventh child. As a girl she lived in Elton and recounted how one evening while returning home a white hen suddenly appeared and fluttered about ahead of her, blocking her path. She tried shooing it away but as this had no effect, she gave it a kick. To her surprise, there was no resistance and her foot passed straight through the feathered phantom. This was concluded to be an ill omen and her father died shortly afterwards.

Where the ancient path crosses a metalled lane, turn sharp right – 3 – away from Elton. Go through a squeeze style and continue diagonally across the field.

Follow the fence line in the next field, then bear right a little to reach and cross the B5056 – 4. Cross the road and follow the path through Oddo Park to reach Winster via the churchyard – 5.

Mr Dennis Slater has twice seen the ghost of a small old lady with a kind, gentle face, crossing the road at the bend below Winster Vicarage, near the approach to what is now the cemetery. At least one other Winster resident has seen the same old lady at the same spot. They all agree that she wears a bonnet and an old fashioned dress and remains visible for as long as the observer can refrain from blinking. The flutter of an eyelid will cause her immediate dissolution.

Turn left via West Bank, then right again along the main village street which is lined with attractive period properties, until you reach Winster Hall, an impressive Georgian house on your left. Built in the 18th century from grit stone brought from Stancliffe Quarries in Darley Dale, it replaced an earlier house built by Francis Moore in 1628. The Moore family were lawyers and mine owners. Llewellyn Jewitt, editor of *The Reliquary*, a famous antiquarian, artist and collector of Derbyshire folklore and legends lived here between 1867-1880. It has since had many uses, including a fire-arms factory, a home for disabled persons during World War II, a public house and restaurant. It is now a private house.

The hall has for many years had a reputation for being haunted by the spectre of a woman linked with a rather tragic love-story. She is believed to be the daughter of the house who, having fallen in love with the coach-man was being forced to marry someone selected by her parents, some-one they considered more suitable for a lady in her position.

Tragically, the night before her wedding, the lovers climbed to the top of the house and clinging to each other, they jumped over the balustrading at the parapet to their deaths. The young lovers were buried opposite the door of Winster church but the wraith of this unhappy girl is still said to haunt the Hall and the forecourt where she met her death.

Winster Hall, haunted by a heartbroken maiden

Continue to walk until reaching the old Market Hall – 6, the first property in the area to be acquired by the National Trust. On your right immediately before this is East Bank and directly opposite on your left is a building that was once the Angel Inn, one of the eighteen inns and taverns in Winster in 1764. Apparently, the name of this establishment belied its reputation and it closed its doors as The Angel in 1916. It is now a private house.

The Old Angel Inn, haunted by a headless bride, stands next to the old Market Hall

A murder supposedly took place in one of the bedrooms, probably a strangulation, as some time ago, a lady sleeping in that room woke, convinced that she was being choked by ghostly hands.

There are accounts of doors opening and closing, and ghostly footsteps, but the most bizarre is the story of the headless bride.

One day a lady at The Angel Inn was sitting at her dressing table concentrating on her reflection. Behind her the door was open and through the looking glass, she had a clear view of the first floor landing and the flight of stairs to the upper floor. Suddenly her attention was diverted from her own reflection to that of a white-clad figure slowly descending the upper flight of stairs to the landing outside her open door. The figure was a young woman dressed as a bride but the most terrifying aspect was the absence of a head, the neck just faded into nothing. As the figure walked un-hesitatingly towards her, the lady at the dressing table fainted.

There appears to be no link with The Angel' and a bride and no explanation as to why this spectre should be headless; beheaded accidentally or otherwise. The Angel'closed its doors as an inn long ago, and the three storey building is now a private residence.

The lady at her dressing table fainted
when a headless bride walked towards her

Turn right into East Bank. Just after the Old Bowling Green Inn on your left is a short stretch leading to one of the most distinctive public conveniences you are likely to encounter. Continue up East Bank which rises steeply around a double bend.

Some of the delightful cottages on East Bank have a paranormal history

Mr and Mrs Dennis Slater lived in a cottage at East Bank, Winster where occasionally they were woken in the night by a series of bumps on the stairs. Going to investigate there was never any reason for the mysterious bumps which were always the same number and regularity. One night when Dennis went to investigate, he tripped and fell down the stairs – the same number of bumps at exactly the same intervals. After that, the Slaters never heard the bumps again.

This cottage had previously been purchased by a sailor who went off to sea and never came back, at least not in the flesh. Often Dennis heard footsteps crossing the bedroom floor, sometimes even when he lay in the bed. Although he never saw anything, his nephew did and described the apparition of a sailor. Another relative scorned the idea until one night she was left in charge of the house while the Slaters were out. When they returned, they found the door open, the lights and TV still switched on and no sign of the relative who later admitted she had heard the ghostly footsteps and freaked.

But it wasnt just footsteps that were heard. On one occasion, a friend had called to watch TV with Dennis, and during the programme he enquired whether Mrs Slater, was upstairs rehearsing as he could hear singing coming from the room above. Dennis assured him his wife was not even in the house but as he listened he too heard someone singing in a clear soprano voice. As he quickly ascended the stairs to investigate, the singing stopped and there was no sign of the singer. What made this incident even more strange was the fact that Mr Slaters friend was quite deaf.

The gradient eventually eases and as you pass the last houses on your left, turn left at a stile – 7. Follow the footpath as it climbs up the field past the heavily wooded heights of Wyn's Tor. Continue beside the wall to reach a walled lane – the Limestone Way – 8. If you turn left you can follow this route to Lunter Rocks.

There are many tales of hauntings associated with these rocks and numerous reports of strange lights seen hovering and dancing over them. These ghost lights have a variety of names locally, like will-o-the-wisp, jack-lantern and St Elmos fire or Ignis Fatuus from Medieval Latin, literally meaning foolish fire. Accounts of ghost lights were common last century in local folklore, but these have decreased at the same rate as the increase in sightings transforming these air-borne lights into flying saucers and UFOs. Explanations for these ghostly rays and beams have come and gone but the lights over rocky outcrops like Lunter Rocks remain.

As you pause to recover your breath take a good look around. Do you see anything moving in the landscape?

Stories of phantom animals that roam the countryside have fired the imagination of countless generations of Peakland folk, and every year even more people report encounters with mysterious creatures. They come in all shapes and sizes, and although many are considered suspect because there is no photographic evidence or bodies, can we dismiss them entirely? Judge for yourself after reading this article which appeared in the *High Peak News* – June 16th 1897.

The most interesting item in natural history, so far as the Matlock district is concerned, transpired this morning, our reporter learns from Mr Roper of Winster, while on Brown Edge, near that village, Mr Roper shot what he thought to be a fox which had been seen in the locality some time previously on Mr Foxlow's land. Thinking he had missed his aim, Mr Roper gave up the quest, but returning later, he found he had killed the animal. It proved to be an extraordinarily large tom-cat, tortoiseshell in colour, with fur two inches and a half long. But what made it remarkable were the remarkable addition of fully-formed pheasant wings projecting from each side of its fourth rib. The animal was exhibited all round the area, but the weather being hot, it began to putrefy and was buried. People who had seen it said that when running the animal used its wings outstretched to help it cover the ground at a tremendous pace.

Winged cats would normally be dismissed as some fantasy animal confined to folk-lore and silly season' tabloid stories were it not for the remarkable fact that they are unquestionably real. In the early 1990's British cryptozoologist Dr Karl Shuker discovered that some cats exhibit a little known genetic disorder known as feline cutaneous asthenia (FCA) which makes the skin extremely stretchable especially on the back, haunches and shoulders. These extensions often contain muscle fibres which allows them to be raised and lowered just like wings.

So next time you hear about flying cats, dont dismiss them as a product of some over active imagination; they are alive and authentic and indisputably living in the Peak District.

Follow the Limestone Way track back down to reach the B5056 opposite the Ore House. Turn right and walk the short distance down the road to the Miners Standard which is the start/end of this walk.

BASLOW – CHATSWORTH PARK – CHATSWORTH HOUSE – EDENSOR – PILSLEY – HASSOP – CALVER – BASLOW
DISTANCE 10 MILES (16·20KM) OR 8 MILES (13KM)

99

Baslow is one of the most picturesque villages of Derbyshire noted for its magnificent position amid moorland and river scenery, and sitting on the northern edge of Chatsworth Park. Our walk begins at the car park by the triangular paddock known as Goose Green, and passes the scenic thatched cottage that is haunted by a previous lady-owner, but that's just for starters. On this walk we encounter sixteen spooky tales.

The overall length can be reduced by 2 miles (3km) if the walk does not include Calver.

To reach Baslow from Bakewell, take the A619 road into Baslow. Go round the roundabout and continue on the A619 towards Chesterfield. After passing the Cavendish Hotel on your right, turn by the triangular paddock known as Goose Green and the pay and display car park is on your right.

THE WALK

Leave the car park in Baslow – 1 – and turn right, following the road over a humped-back bridge to pass in front of a haunted thatched cottage.

One day, a tramp called at a thatched cottage in Baslow begging for food, and although she was cooking bacon for herself at the time, the lady of the house told him she had no food for lazy ruffians like himself. This so incensed the tramp that he forced his way inside, grabbed the pan and poured the boiling fat down her throat, scalding her to death.

The haunted thatched cottage

Following his arrest and trial, he was sentenced to be hung in chains from a gibbet erected on Gibbet Moor just off the main Baslow/Chesterfield road, to die a slow and painful death. Well-meaning people brought him food but that just prolonged his agony. His screams were said to have so upset the Duke of Devonshire at Chatsworth House directly west of Gibbet Moor, that he brought about the legislation to prohibit such an inhuman practice.

This unknown tramp was the last person in England to be gibbeted alive and the poor man's screams are still heard. In July 1992 Jane Townsend reported hearing what she described as bloodcurdling and petrifying screams while hiking in the area of Gibbet Moor.

But this is a double haunting. The cottage at Baslow is also said to be haunted by the murdered woman. According to the late Edgar Osbourne, a retired librarian and archivist at Chatsworth House who lived in the cottage, during times of illness when he was in much pain, the old woman appeared at his bedside and soothed him. Poor recompense for the way she refused the tramp!

Just past the thatched cottages, go through a metal squeeze stile on the left of a gate, then follow the wide gravel path straight on, skirting to the left round Plantation Cottage to reach a rather unusual revolving metal gate – 2. This allows wheelchair access to Chatsworth Park and was the inspiration of Mrs Jill Cannon who gave it the name Cannon Kissing Gate. It was made and donated by Mathers Engineering of Tibshelf and was opened by the Duke of Devonshire and Mrs Cannon on March 17th 1999.

The unusual revolving gate known as the Cannon Kissing Gate designed for wheelchair users

Chatsworth Park extends to over 450 hectares on both sides of the River Derwent and is open to the public almost in its entirety. We are heading south along the well trodden path sign posted Chatsworth House, Queen Mary's Bower.

In 1549 Bess of Hardwick and her second husband Sir William Cavendish bought the manor of Chatsworth and built a mansion house which has been added to and changed by subsequent generations of the Cavendish family whose home it has been for 460 years. Chatsworth House, which you will see on your left as you continue this walk is undoubtedly one of England's finest stately homes and is often referred to as The Palace of the Peak.

Follow the path, going straight on at the crossroads of lanes/tracks beside White Lodge gatehouse for a further ¾ mile. This is part of the Derwent Valley Heritage Way. Just before reaching the access road to Chatsworth House, note the stone building on your immediate left. This is Queen Mary's Bower, the haunt of Mary, Queen of Scots and one of the few buildings that date back to the Elizabethan Chatsworth.

It has been claimed that Mary Queen of Scots is Derbyshire's most prolific phantom, but that's probably due to the injustices she suffered while here. She first arrived in Derbyshire in March 1565, but it wasnt for a visit. Two months earlier she had been placed under house arrest in the custody of the 6th Earl of Shrewsbury and his wife Bess of Hardwick at Tutbury Castle on the Derbyshire/Staffordshire border. From there, she was moved to Wingfield Manor and shortly afterwards to Chatsworth House. Several times she was transported to Buxton to take the curative waters and as the Earl and Countess were to remain her captors until 1584 during all those years she was constantly moved around their palatial Derbyshire homes. She was imprisoned five times at Chatsworth House.

The royal status of the captive queen assured her of considerable privileges, except for the one thing she wanted most – freedom to wander around out of doors. As a slight concession, a belvedere was built in the grounds near the River Derwent. This single storey structure with blank stone walls is topped with a flat roof surrounded by a wall, broken in places by stone balustrading. The design is rather like a raised play-pen where the captive Queen could wonder to while away those long summer days. It was used for picnics as well as providing a grandstand for any entertainment in the grounds, but its main purpose as a prison was never in doubt. As a further precautionary step, the whole was surrounded by a moat and entered by a steep flight of stone steps. The design of this moated belvedere allowed Mary to spend considerable time in the open while still enclosed behind restricting walls with a substantial locked door or gate over which were Mary's initials and coat of arms.

Writing in '*The Estate – A View from Chatsworth*' the Dowager Duchess of Devonshire explains that the raised enclosure was built on the site of an ancient earthwork and adds – The building itself was largely restored by Wyatville in 1823-4 but its old bones are clearly visible in the thick walls and the broad flight of steps over the now dry moat.'

Queen Mary's Bower,
haunted by the unhappy Queen

To mark the 400th anniversary of the death of Bess of Hardwick, the bower was opened for daylight viewing in 2008, so I felt very privileged to be allowed to walk around the top, the entire surface of which is covered in meadow grass.

I was able to look out over the stone balustrade which documents date from 1581, and although the views are striking, the trees are now much too large to enjoy the same panorama that the Elizabethan visitors could. An added bonus was that all the recent rain had filled the moat.

Although I was aware that Mary Queen of Scots' unhappy spirit is said to walk around the area immediately in front of the building before ascending the steps and disappearing, sadly I didnt see her.

Apparently the ill-fated Queen is seen surrounded by an azure light and always has a dejected look about her.

Leave Queen Mary's Bower, and proceed to the haunted bridge over the River Derwent – 3. Millions of people pass over this stone bridge leading to Chatsworth House without really noticing it. Photographers walk slightly upstream to photograph the bridge with Chatsworth House in the background, but few give even a cursory glance at the other side where two stone statues adorn it. They are hardly a matching pair – one is a man holding a child on his shoulders, the other a classic male statue. The latter replaced a statue of a woman that fell into the water and was never retrieved, which is a shame because the original statues were said to be a sad reminder of a dreadful deed that happened in the 18th century.

Two servants working at Chatsworth House formed a liaison which blossomed into full union. The girl Frances Coulton became pregnant and gave birth to a baby boy. Immediately after the birth, the father, James Loton of Edensor, appeared on the scene, swept the new-born infant into his arms and ran towards the river. Pursued by the distraught mother, he paused at the bridge crossing the River Derwent, then threw the babe into the water.

The statues on Chatsworth bridge that originally told such a poignant story

According to a report at the time – In March 22nd 1739, James Loton was found guilty at Derbyshire Assizes of the murder of a male bastard child. Frances Coulton gave evidence against him, because charged with the same offence, she turned King's evidence and was accordingly acquitted. Lord Chief Baron Page sentenced Loton to be hanged, but no fewer than six times over the following months, his sentence was respited. Accounts of the trial stated that he was a man of good standing, and probably more relevant under the circumstances, he was a man of considerable substance. Finally in August, he was eventually given a pardon and allowed to return home.

But the crime is not totally forgotten, as the bridge has a reputation of being haunted. Walkers have been stopped in their tracks by the agonizing cries of the young mother who is said to haunt the bridge and river banks searching for her newborn child. What is equally distressing are the claims of people who have reported the gurgling gasps of the drowning baby.

With your back to Chatsworth House, leave the bridge and almost immediately branch off to the right on the gravel path which gradually leaves the road and reaches the main B6012 road which runs through Chatsworth Park, opposite Edensor. Over to your left is a solitary cottage in the dip which is all that is left of the original 1740 village of Edensor. The 6th Duke of Devonshire objected to the village being visible from Chatsworth House and had it demolished and rebuilt on its present site, all except the single solitary cottage with the intriguing name of Naboth's Vineyard. The name comes from the bible story in the first book of Kings XXI.

Naboth owned a vineyard which was sited next to the royal palace of Ahab, king of Samaria. Ahab was rich, powerful and owned much land but he also wanted Naboth's vineyard. He offered him money, but Naboth refused; he offered him another vineyard but Naboth refused that stating – 'I will not give thee the inheritance of my fathers.'

This did not please Ahab, but he was married to the wicked Jezebel who plotted to have Naboth killed so that Ahab could then take possession, but the Lord was not pleased and brought evil upon his house.

When the 6th Duke destroyed the remainder of Edensor did the owner of this delightful little cottage compare this to the action of Ahab and thus saved his cottage?

Cross the road by the cattle grid and go through the gates into the model estate village of Edensor (pronounced Ensor) – 4.

The entrance to Edensor.
The quaint Post Office which also
serves refreshment – that you can share
with a spaniel called Jay

105

*Edensor –
the main village street*

It is well worth a visit to St Peter's Church to see the monuments and graves of the Cavendish family, but perhaps the most surprising is that of Kathleen Kennedy, sister of John F Kennedy the American President. Kathleen was the wife of William Cavendish who should have inherited the estate and title of Duke of Devonshire had he not been killed in the Second World War. Four years later, in 1948 at the age of twenty eight Kathleen was killed in a plane crash.

Leave the church and take the road passing in front of the church which becomes unsuitable for motorists as you leave Edensor. When the lane forks, take the left hand stony track and follow this, climbing steadily for ¾ mile to reach Handley Lane – 5. Turn right along Handley Lane and continue for about ¾ mile until reaching the B6048 – 6. From here there are great views over Handley Bottom to your left.

Cross the road and take the footpath opposite over the stile. The path veers slightly to the right across the field to reach a wall stile and the entrance to a grassy lane. Continue straight ahead ignoring the left branch. The lane curves round to the right to join a gravel track on the outskirts of Pilsley – 7.

One night, a police dog-handler was driving along the road heading towards Pilsley when a figure appeared in the full beam of the headlights. Although the officer braked furiously he couldnt avoid hitting him head on.

The man bounced over the bonnet and fell. In a state of shock, the officer grabbed a torch and jumped out of his van. He released his dog who jumped out, howled pitifully and shot off down the road.

The officer searched the roadside looking for the accident victim but there was no-one and the hedge was undisturbed. He checked the front of the vehicle for signs of the impact, but could see nothing. He got back inside the van and proceeded slowly down the road just to make sure the injured person hadnt somehow stumbled away from the scene of the accident. As he drove he realised that although he had seen the impact he hadnt felt it or heard it.

At first light, he returned to the scene of the accident but could find no trace of anything strange. Back at the police station, he began to explain what had happened but the Sergeant stopped him. Dont worry about it,' he said. 'A man was killed at that spot many years ago and the replay is witnessed regularly.'

We continue our walk on the sign posted track on your left, but first, why not explore the delightful estate village of Pilsley with its cluster of 18th and 19th century stone houses with the blue livery of the Chatsworth Estate.

The estate village of Pilsley

Centuries ago, this was a busy place where several important pack-horse routes converged. To cater for this trade, in 1835 the village had three alehouses and two inns. Now just the Devonshire Arms remains. There is only one post office/shop but continue up past the primary school on your right to where the road meets the main B6048. Cross

107

the road and walk up the short lane opposite which leads to Chatsworth Farm Shop. This was the old Stud Farm but now it's a Mecca for locals and visitors who appreciate good quality local food.

Return to the previously mentioned track on the other side of Pilsley and follow it, heading down hill to meet the A619, Bakewell – Baslow Road – 9.

> A man regularly drove along the A619 road from Baslow to Bakewell and on many occasions saw an old man leaning on a five bar gate, smoking a pipe. This same old man seemed to appear so frequently that it became much more than just a coincidence. He was a ghost, so in death it would appear that this old man was doing what he had done in his lifetime.

Turn right along the road for 50 yards then take the stony track through a gate, sign posted 'Unsuitable for Motorists'. On reaching another gate continue straight ahead, at first with Toost Bank Woods your right, then through Birchin Bank Wood. Remain on this track, over an old clapper bridge that crosses the Rymas Brook, past the edge of a farmyard to join the B6001 at Hassop – 8.

> There are many stories told about the stretch of road between Hassop station and village. It could be the most haunted road in Derbyshire. One gentleman who regularly travelled on this route, said that as he passed Hassop Hall Lodge and former Dower House he was often aware of the scent of honeysuckle. Pleasant though this was, it was rather disturbing to smell such a scent in mid winter.

One gentleman was often aware of a scent of honeysuckle around here

Ash House between Bakewell and Hassop is a small round stone building once used as a store for blocks of potash, prepared nearby and sent away for use in glass making. One old tale refers to a shepherd who made this little hut his home and reputedly hid his meagre savings between slabs in the stone roof. A thief, intent upon robbing the poor shepherd climbed on the roof which gave way under his weight, killing himself, the shepherd and his dog. If you listen, they say you can occasionally still hear the old shepherd whistling his dog.

If you travel along the Bakewell to Hassop road, dont be surprised if you encounter a phantom cavalier who supposedly steps out into the road in front of vehicles, or the phantom coach and horses that is likely to overtake you. Many motorists who have encountered them suffer from shock, and apparently one died after swerving to avoid crashing into a coach and horses crossing his path Traumatized people who have witnessed these strange phenomena call in the Eyre Arms in Hassop to tell their stories, and they all bear a striking similarity. What few realise is that the cavalier also haunts the Eyre Arms where he has appeared to customers and staff. Phantom coaches are customarily black, pulled by headless black horses and driven at a furious pace by a driver with skeletal or grotesque features. There is a belief that they are often seen prior to a death in the family, or alternatively anyone who gets in the way of a phantom coach will be carried away to their own doom. See also the phantom coach that runs between Youlgreave and Middleton on Walk 3.

A Sheffield man was driving home from Bakewell one night. He was driving slowly to negotiate several bends in the road near Hassop Hall when suddenly there was a blinding flash and his car engine just stopped. He sat for a few minutes quite dazed, then tried restarting the engine but it appeared to be quite dead. In frustration, he opened the car door and was met by an icy blast of cold air. He shivered as he went round to release the bonnet catch and peer at the engine. There was no smoke or smell of burning which might have explained the flash, so he closed the bonnet and got back into the car. The engine started up immediately and he drove on rather warily.

A few minutes later he was passing the Eyre Arms and noticed a police-man riding a cycle ahead of him. He decided to enquire if the patrolling officer had seen anything unusual, but the policeman turned right into the

109

narrow Wheatlands Lane. The driver deciding it was not that urgent, and proceeded on his way to Calver. Some time later, he met the police officer who patrolled the area and decided to mention the incident. The officer stared at him in surprise. Police officers no longer rode around on bicycles, they carried out their patrol duties in panda cars.

Turn right along this haunted stretch of road and watch out! Follow it through Hassop, an attractive mixture of farms and cottages centred around the gates to Hassop Hall.

Hidden away behind a tall garden wall in the tranquil village of Hassop between Bakewell and Calver is Hassop Hall. Its now a very popular country house hotel but the recorded history of Hassop reaches back 900 years when it was the principle residence of the Foljambes who remained until the end of the 14th century. The last of the Foljambes was an 11 month old infant heiress who became a ward of the King. He sold her for 50 marks to Sir John Leake, who promptly made 100% profit by re-selling her for 100 marks to Sir William Plumpton as a bride for his son. With the infant heiress went a considerable dowry which included Hassop.

At the close of the 15th century, Hassop came into the ownership of the Eyre family, until in 1852, Francis Eyre, the 8th Earl of Newburgh died unmarried. The estate then passed to his sister who was also childless and on her death, it became the property of her widower, Colonel Charles Leslie. He may have inherited the estate but not the title and this became a contested affair.

A Mr Cadman of Sheffield claimed he was a descendant but this was refuted. The claim by Maria Bandini Giustiniani was allowed and she became the countess in 1858. Upon her death in 1877 her son became the 9th Earl. In the 1880s there was another claimant on the scene. A Gladwin Clovers Cave came over from Australia to claim the estate and take the Hall by force, but his claim was also unsubstantiated.

During all of this time, tales had been circulating about the old beech tree that stood in the grounds of Hassop Hall. It was said to be an oracle tree, able to predict the name of the rightful owner. With so much at stake its not surprising that various would-be owners tried to chop it down, but no sooner had they lifted the axe when some weird, unfortunate accident occurred. One man alleged that the tree warned that the house itself would fall if the tree was ever cut down by human hands.

Although this might now sound rather bizarre, the association of trees with wisdom and knowledge was common in many cultures and religions.

It was an ancient belief that trees were inhabited by the gods who gave them powers to foretell many things. From the early Druids onwards, wise men would sit under specific trees and interpret the rustling of the leaves and other subtle signs as oracular messages.

It was said that when the wind blew from the west, the Hassop beech tree would whisper the name of the rightful owner of the Hassop estate and the words – 'All Hail, true heir that stills my voice.'

A combination of age and weather ultimately tore down the tree, but the ownership is no longer in question. It has been in the hands of the present owner Thomas Chapman and his family since 1975.

And for good measure, another sighting of that phantom coach was experienced early one morning by a guest staying at Hassop Hall. He looked out of his bedroom window and saw a coach and horses being driven along the drive. It looked so impressive, when the guest went down for breakfast he asked the receptionist if it was possible to book the coach for a nostalgic drive around the area. The receptionist looked puzzled. It is possible to book a period coach for such an event through Red Horse Stables at Darley Dale, (*see Walk 4*) but after making a thorough check, the guest was informed that no such coach had called at Hassop Hall that morning.

A phantom coach travels along this stretch of road past the Eyre Arms and has been seen at Hassop Hall

Bear round to the right towards Calver, and the Eyre Arms on your left – 9. The Eyre Arms at Hassop has what is called a 'lepers sill' in a former outer wall at the rear of the building. When during the Middle

111

Ages, the dreadful disease of leprosy left people with terrible disfigurations, sufferers were compelled to ring a bell to broadcast their approach and hide their hideous deformities under a hooded cloak. The leper's sill is purportedly where leper's could be served away from and out of sight of healthier drinkers.

Turn right into School Lane – 10 – signposted to Baslow. Follow this road gently dropping down into a shallow valley then rising and bending to the right past the entrance of Ox Pasture Farm. Continue along School Lane until the woodland ends on your left where you find a wall stile just after a gate – 11. If you prefer to take the shorter option, continue down School Lane which becomes Wheatlands Lane and resume the walk at the bridge over the River Derwent in Baslow – point 15.

To continue the full walk, follow the signed footpath, bearing left across a field alongside the field boundary/woodland on your left to reach a stile in the top left corner. Cross the stile and follow the path straight on along the top of a steep, wooded bank with a wall on your right. The path leads through Bank Wood South. It then clears to offer views towards Longstone Edge, before passing through Bank Wood North. The footpath is bisected by Bramley Lane which you cross to take the footpath opposite/left. Follow this along the edge of Bramley Wood on your left and a wall on your right, heading along the top of the wooded ridge for almost ½ mile.

As you approach the end of the ridge, a wonderful bird's eye view of Calver unfolds – 12 – before you begin to descend. Where the wall on your right bends away, carry straight on down through woodland to reach a junction of paths. Head left for a few paces, then follow the clear path bending sharply down to the left across the wooded hillside. Where this path forks after a short distance, follow the obvious path bending to the right steeply down across the sparsely wooded hillside to reach a stile tucked away in the fence corner at the bottom of the wooded bank. Cross the stile and follow the path straight on across the field down into a shallow valley. The path then rises to join a wall on your right. Follow this until you reach a stile that leads onto an enclosed path on the edge of Calver. Ignore the path off to the right, to soon join a gravel driveway. Follow to the left then the right through the former farmyard of Folds Farm to reach Shippon Lane at the end of which is the Main Street through Calver village – 13.

Calver High Street. At the end is the Victorian lamp standard

Turn right to reach the triangular road junction in the heart of the village with a Victorian lamp standard commemorating Queen Victoria's coronation on June 28th 1838. Just before the lamp, take Lowside which runs off to the left, and on your right is the Derwent Water Arms.

The Derwent Water Arms, the haunt of a former landlord

113

Many years ago, a landlord of the Derwent Water Arms was in the habit of playing practical jokes. One evening he lay on the parlour table and got his wife to cover him with a sheet. She was then instructed to go into the bar and tell his customers he had died suddenly.

Naturally the customers expressed their condolences and the wife invited them into the parlour to pay their respects to the corpse! They gathered round the table in a sympathetic silence then suddenly the deceased'sat up and terrified his audience. But fate was about to take a hand. The following day the landlord was driving to Bakewell in his horse-drawn trap when the horse suddenly shied. The man was thrown and broke his neck, so that evening, he actually lay on the same table, but this time he was a genuine corpse.

Various landlords have since reported hearing unexplained footsteps and being aware of an inexplicable presence. Regular visitors would not stay in one of the bedrooms and in order to find out why, a landlady and her niece slept in there one night. They occupied the double bed and a maid had a single bed in the corner. All was well until the bewitching hour of midnight when the door opened and a menacing presence entered the room. It stopped to view the occupants walked round the bed, paused, then left the room. Could it be the ghost of that landlord playing another of his practical jokes?

Return to the Victorian lamp stand and turn right into Main Street. Continue until passing the Primitive Methodist Chapel on your left, then on your right is the Village Hall in front of which is a small brook. Take the enclosed path immediately after the entrance to the Village Hall, squeezed in between the car park and the neighbouring house.

It's quite narrow but opens up at a gate into a field. Follow the path across the fields to join the riverside path along the banks of the River Derwent.

The Primitive Methodist Chapel

After passing through St Mary's Wood, the broad path curves round to the left following a curve in the river, then bears to the right away from the river. Head along the foot of a wooded bank then onto a wide path until reaching a gate. Follow the path as it bears slightly right. Pass through a squeeze stile and follow the path through a field to a roadside gate.

You have now reached Bubnell Lane – 14. Turn left and continue along this lane for ⅔ mile (1km) through the hamlet of Bubnell until reaching the Old Bridge across the River Derwent that leads into the Bridge End area of Baslow – 15. If you have opted for the shorter walk this is where you will resume this walk.

The footpath next to the village hall leads to the river

The old bridge is where the river was originally crossed at a ford, then a wooden bridge. According to early records, there were complaints that this narrow bridge was suffering constant damage for excessively heavy loads. As a result in 1500 it was ordered that *'from henceforth no one shall carry or lead any millstones over the bridge at Basselowe under pain of 6s8d to the lord for every pair of millstones so carried'*.

The bridge over the River Derwent with the tiny toll hut

The wooden bridge was replaced in 1603 by the present three arched bridge. What makes this so unusual is the tiny toll hut which offered shelter for a watchman who would guard this important river crossing and collect tolls for the privilege.

115

Cross the bridge and turn right. On your right is St Anne's Church with its squat spire, battlemented parapets and unusual clock face with VICTORIA 1897 rather than numerals. This was to commemorate the Queen's Diamond Jubilee. A visit to St Anne's Church is advisable but before entering pause at the porch.

There was an old belief in many rural areas that if you sat in the church porch on the evening of Halloween (some churches favoured April 24th – St Mark's Eve) you would see a procession of the wraiths of the people who would die during the following year. Every Halloween, William Cundy the local wise-man, (*see Walk 8*) sat in the porch of St Anne's Church, Baslow, and watched for the procession of the dead. Did he see himself, because according to the Baslow Parish register, William Cundy died at the age of 73 and was buried on February 16th 1856.

There's also an early folktale that relates to Baslow church porch and first appeared in print in 1526. One evening two young thieves were intent upon stealing a sheep from the meadows by the side of the river and while one went to locate a suitable animal, his accomplice concealed himself in the church porch. To pass the time while he waited, he began to crack and eat a bag of nuts he had in his pocket.

It was drawing dusk and the sexton was hurrying up the church path, anxious to get to the church to ring the nightly curfew bell, but he stopped in his stride and listened because in the gloom of the deserted churchyard he could see nothing, yet the sound of splintering and munching carried clearly on the still night air.

'Tis the devil himself, devouring wayward souls,' he cried turning on his heel and running back down the path. Heaven knows there are enough in this parish!'

He ran all the way to the vicarage muttering a protective prayer to himself, but when the vicar heard the sexton's tale, he laughed. He didnt share the sexton's superstitious ideas and tried to reassure him that there would be an obvious solution that didnt involve the devil. But the sexton could not be convinced and refused to return to the church alone. Under normal circumstances, the vicar would have returned with the sexton just to clarify the situation, but his gout was playing up and the poor man was in such pain he was hardly able to put his feet to the ground. This presented the vicar with a problem because if the sexton refused to return, the curfew bell would not be rung so a compromise was needed. Eventually they agreed that the sexton should carry the vicar on his back, and off they went.

With his knees buckling under the weight of the portly vicar, the sexton made his way slowly towards the church. He was bent almost double as he staggered along the church path, grunting and groaning under his heavy load. Hearing this, the youth concealed in the church porch thought it was his companion returning with a stolen sheep and called out eagerly – Is it a fat un?'

'Aye, an'tha can tek it, if tha likes!'cried the sexton as he tipped the vicar onto the floor and ran.

Deserted by the sexton and with what he imagined was the Devil approaching him, the vicar forgot his gout, picked himself up and followed the sexton. Both men locked themselves in their homes and prayed all night for deliverance.

Meanwhile the second thief returned with a fine, fat sheep slung over his shoulders and the two youths departed leaving only a pile of nut shells for the shame-faced sexton to find next morning.

Baslow church porch where the Devil devoured wayward souls

Before entering the church note the remains of a sanctuary knocker on the door. In earlier centuries, any criminal could claim refuge inside a church and was safe the moment he touched that sanctuary knocker.

Inside the Church of St Anne is a very unusual find, a dog whip preserved in a glass fronted, wooden case that hangs just inside the main door. The lash is about three feet long and secured to a stout stick of ash with leather bound handle. Dog whips were regularly in use in our parish churches for many centuries and the Church warders account at Youlgreave Parish Church included the salary of the dog-whipper and makes interesting reading.

1609 – *To Robert Walton for whipping ye dogges forthe of ye churche in tyme of divyne service'– one shilling and four pence*.(6-7p)

1617 – *To Robert Benbowe for whipping out y dogges – two shillings.* (10p)

1715 – *For a coat and furniture for y dog-whipper – eleven shillings and six pence.* (57 ½ p)

The need for such precautions seems to have stemmed from a legend at Bungay in Suffolk that a demonic black dog, wide-eyed and salivating, entered the church on Sunday August 4th 1577 when most of the town-folk were at prayer. Te dog was probably rabid because it killed two people and injuring a third. To prevent this happening elsewhere, churches employed dog-whippers to keep rabid animals out of church. There could also be another reason.

According to tradition, the first person to be buried in a graveyard returned in spirit to protect the dead from the devil, demons and other nefarious supernatural creatures that might haunt such places, so before any human was interred, a black dog would be buried alive in the grounds of a newly built church, thus creating a canine guardian spirit, known as the kirke-grim or church grim.

We know the job of the church-grim was to protect and guard the grave-yard, but could it also have taken on the role of protecting the church, and be the reason why it was necessary to have a dog whip handy?

Leave the church and turn right along Church Street to the round-about Go straight across into Church Lane which runs into Cock Hill. On your right after passing the Cavendish Hotel, turn by the triangular paddock known as Goose Green and you are back at the car park which is the start/end of this walk.

8: Robin Hood, Dragons, Aristocratic Apparitions and Blood Curdling Screams

BIRCHEN EDGE – NELSON'S MONUMENT – WELLINGTON'S MONUMENT – THE EAGLE STONE – BASLOW – CHATSWORTH – ROBIN HOOD
Distance 7 Miles – (11·35 km)

Chatsworth House is surrounded by 1,000 acres of parkland that originally formed the western boundary of Sherwood Forest. It still has many ancient oak trees as well as herds of roaming deer, so would you be surprised to find that on its northern edge is a hamlet named after the famous outlaw of Sherwood Forest – Robin Hood? This tiny hamlet consists of the Robin Hood Inn, Robin Hood Farm and Robin Hood Plantation. We can't guarantee that you will encounter the world's most famous outlaw, but you could stumble upon the fire eating dragon that destroyed Leash Fen, some local traditions and ghostly tales.

To reach Robin Hood from Bakewell, take the A619 road to Baslow. Go round the roundabout and continue on the A619 towards Chesterfield. Pass through Baslow and at the next roundabout continue on the A619 towards Chesterfield for one mile (1·50km) until reaching the B6050 on your left. The Robin Hood pub is on the left, set back from the road, as it straddles the junction of the B6050 with the A619. Turn into the B6050 and park in the Birchin Edge car park adjoining the Robin Hood pub car park – map reference 281:722.

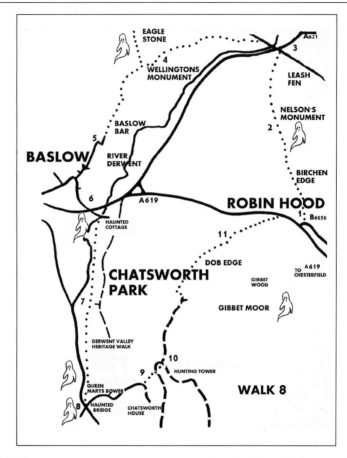

The hamlet of Robin Hood – Robin Hood Inn and Robin Hood Farm

THE WALK

Leave the Birchin Edge car park –1 – and turn left up the B6050. Pass Robin Hood Farm on your left then leave the road, turning left to walk up the bank to go through a five bar gate.

The path is marked but it can get rather overgrown

Keep straight on up the wide steps, following the well-used sand and rock path uphill round to the left following the garden wall. Pass the nine hole golf course on your left, ignoring the path on the right and continue, ignoring another smaller path on the right. And follow the rocky path below Birchin Edge.

According to an ancient almost forgotten tale, a dragon had a lair on Birchin Edge, and like all good dragon stories, this dragon was a personification of the devil who laid waste to the land and sizzled up the countryside with its fiery breath. But it wasnt just countryside. On the edge of Birchin Edge was a town called Leash Fen, so what chance had the wooden huts of Leash Fen against a monster breathing huge tongues of flame?

Fortunately help was at hand in the shape of a hermit who climbed Winlatter Rock, the highest point on Birchin Edge and held up his arms in the

The fire-breathing dragon destroyed the town of Leash Fen

121

shape of a cross. The dragon attacked, but the hermit stood so firm his feet sunk into the rock and held him upright. The dragon was overcome! As news of the triumph spread, people flocked to the rock to look at the two foot holes and Birchin Edge became a place of pilgrimage. It was believed that only the bravest heroes or a person helped by the gods could succeed in destroying a dragon, but on this occasion, the deed was only delayed.

The dragon made another attempt but this time was challenged by three brothers who fashioned a huge silver sword which they erected on the same spot. Silver defeats evil because it is a symbol of purity and hope, and the sword, held with its hilt upwards like a cross had strong Christian significance.

The fiend with its sharp teeth and claws, swooped in on huge webbed wings, which gave it the power to fly, despite its heavy, scaly body and long tail, but the boys stood firm. The church bells rang, lightening struck the sword and the disorientated dragon, overcome by a power greater than its own, flew off in the direction of Castleton. He disappeared down Peak Cavern, the largest natural cave-entrance in the British Isle which from that day on became known as The Devils Arse.

The lost town of Leash Fen is still marked on maps. A flat 700 acres site, it is one of the most desolate and least frequented places in Derbyshire and gets its name from the Old English lecc' meaning stream and fenn' a marsh. Little grows there except marsh grasses, some heather and a few scrubby trees, but in the late 1830s, a drainage trench was dug across the middle of the marsh and in the process, *'many pieces of black oak, squared and cut by some instrument'* were found along with some fragments of rude earthenware and coinage. Similar signs of early civilization were later uncovered during excavation for an electricity power line, yet no detailed description or precise location for these finds was ever specified.

In the fen area early dwelling places or huts would almost certainly have been built on piles, which would tie in with the many pieces of squared black oak found buried, yet no further excavation has been done so the mystery of Leash Fen lives on. Is this a lost town? Some credence is given to the legend by an ancient rhyme;-

When Chesterfield was heath and broom,
Leash Fen was a market town.
Now Leash Fen is all heath and broom
and Chesterfield is a market town.

As for the hermits foot holes....the elements have taken their toll, yet we are left with the tantalizing knowledge that in days of old when knights were bold – theres every possibility that dragons roamed Derbyshire.

Continue along this path and soon you will see Nelson's Monument – 2 – up to your right, perched on the top of the Edge 1,000ft above sea level. It was erected in 1810, in memory of Admiral Lord Nelson (1758-1805) and the Battle of Trafalgar in which he died along with over 1,580 fellow sailors. The gritstone shaft is topped with a stone finial ball and each side of the obelisk faces a cardinal point of the compass. The eastern side is inscribed A.D Nelson. Died Oct. 21st 1805. On the opposite side, John Brightman the stonemason left his initials.

Behind the monuments are three large rocks known as the Three Ships. They represent the famous British ships in that battle; their names – Victory – Defiant and Royal Soverin (*sic*) are carved into each rock.

Continue along the edge to a white pillar known as a trig point or triangulation point. Trig points were set up by the Ordnance Survey after 1845 on numerous sites in Britain to enable them to survey the country and hence provide maps. Today trig points are no longer used as aerial and satellite photography provides far more accurate mapping details.

Near the northern end of Birchen Edge the path veers left away from the edge and winds its way down through the purple flowering heather much loved by Derbyshire bees. Very little grows up here but as you follow the path north the ground can become very marshy and sedge grasses and rushes take the place of the heather.

The quaint little bridge over the Bar Brook and the road that leads to Calver

The marshy land where very little grows

This footpath comes out at the junction of Clodhall Lane and the A621 Sheffield/Baslow Road. Cross the road with care and head directly up the hill, pausing at the quaint old bridge that crosses the Bar Brook. After about 100 yards, go through a gate beside a field gate and follow the tractor tracks along Eaglestone Flat.

Heed the notices

Keep straight on the well defined track along the edge to the Wellington Monument – 4 – which you will reach after about ¾ mile. This cross was erected in 1866 by Mr Wrench a Baslow doctor who had previously served as an army surgeon in the Crimean War and India. As the name implies, it is in memory of the Duke of Wellington (1769-1852) of wellington boot fame and his famous victories, particularly the Battle of Waterloo.

On the southern end of Baslow Edge behind the monument is a large rock known as the Eagle Stone.

The Eagle Stone

Whichever way you view it, this huge pile of deformed gritstone has none of the characteristic features of an eagle. In fact anything less bird like than a solid clump of rock is hard to imagine until you realise that Eagle is a corruption of Aigle, the Saxon god who could throw stones that no mortal could move. A local tradition was for the young men of Baslow to climb to the top of the Eagle stone to prove their prowess in some kind of initiation ceremony. They no doubt hoped that in exchange for this show of pubescent bravado, they would be rewarded with some of Aigles mighty strength.

William Cundy was a Baslow wise-man who studied astronomy, astrology and spiritualism. In times of need the villagers went to him for help and advice and he would regularly dispense herbal remedies to cure people and animals. (see also *Walk 7*) One day a child went missing and despite a thorough search of the immediate vicinity, she could not be found. In desperation the family asked William Cundy for his help and after meditating and making various calculations, he announced his findings. He confidently told them that they would find the child asleep in the shadow of the Eagle Stone on Baslow edge with her bonnet by her side. The father rushed to the stone and found his daughter just as Cundy had predicted.

Walkers following a path north below Baslow Edge, may come across a cluster of burial slabs lying flat on the ground. Each is carved with the initials of one of the Cundy family from nearby Grislowfields Farm who died within days of each other when the plague struck Curbar in 1632.

To continue our walk, we follow the track that descends towards Baslow, following the wide stony track downhill. Go through a gate and continue down, following the path down the right hand side of a field wall which in places is broken and replaced by wire fencing. After nearly ½ mile you will meet the surfaced road of Bar Road on the edge of Baslow – 5.

Continue down Bar Road ignoring side roads until reaching a grass island at the junction of School Lane and Bar Road. Turn to the left into Eaton Hill and walk down the hill to reach the main A619 – 6 – and cross the road to Goose Green. The next part of the walk goes into

Chatsworth Park and is identical to the route taken in Walk 7.

Skirt Goose Green and turn left, following the road over a humped back bridge to veer right passing in front of a haunted thatched cottage.

One day, a tramp called at a thatched cottage in Baslow begging for food, and although she was cooking bacon for herself at the time, the lady of the house told him she had no food for lazy ruffians like himself. This so incensed the tramp that he forced his way inside, grabbed the pan and poured the boiling fat down her throat, scalding her to death.

The haunted thatched cottage

Following his arrest and trial, he was sentenced to be hung in chains from a gibbet erected on Gibbet Moor just off the main Baslow/Chesterfield road, to die a slow and painful death. Well-meaning people brought him food but that just prolonged his agony. His screams were said to have so upset the Duke of Devonshire at Chatsworth House directly west of Gibbet Moor, that he brought about the legislation to prohibit such an inhuman practice.

This unknown tramp was the last person in England to be gibbeted alive and the poor man's screams are still heard. In July 1992 Jane Townsend reported hearing what she described as bloodcurdling and petrifying screams while hiking in the area of Gibbet Moor.

But this is a double haunting. The cottage at Baslow is also said to be haunted by the murdered woman. According to the late Edgar Osbourne, a retired librarian and archivist at Chatsworth House who lived in the cottage, during times of illness when he was in much pain, the old woman appeared at his bedside and soothed him. Poor recompense for the way she refused the tramp!

Just past the thatched cottages, go through a metal squeeze stile on the left of a gate, then follow the wide gravel path straight on, skirting to the left round Plantation Cottage to reach a rather unusual revolving metal gate which allows wheelchair access to Chatsworth Park. This was the inspiration of Mrs Jill Cannon who gave it the name Cannon Kissing Gate. It was made and donated by Mathers Engineering of Tibshelf and was opened by the Duke of Devonshire and Mrs Cannon on March 17th 1999. Take the well trodden path straight ahead.

Chatsworth Park extends to over 450 hectares on both sides of the River Derwent and is open to the public almost in its entirety. In 1549 Bess of Hardwick and her second husband Sir William Cavendish bought the manor of Chatsworth and built a mansion house which has been added to and changed by subsequent generations of the Cavendish family whose home it has been for 460 years. It is undoubtedly one of England's finest stately homes and is often referred to as The Palace of the Peak.

Follow the path, and at the crossroads of lanes/tracks beside White Lodge gatehouse – 7 – continue straight on along the Derwent Valley Heritage Way. Just before reaching the access road to Chatsworth House, note the stone building on your immediate left. This is Queen Mary's Bower, the haunt of Mary, Queen of Scots and one of the few buildings that date back to the Elizabethan Chatsworth.

It has been claimed that Mary Queen of Scots is Derbyshire's most prolific phantom, but thats probably due to the injustices she suffered while here. She first arrived in Derbyshire in March 1565, but it wasnt for a visit. Two months earlier she had been placed under house arrest in the custody of the 6th Earl of Shrewsbury and his wife Bess of Hardwick at Tutbury Castle on the Derbyshire/Staffordshire border. From there, she was moved to Wingfield Manor and shortly afterwards to Chatsworth House. Several times she was transported to Buxton to take the curative waters and as the Earl and Countess were to remain her captors until 1584 during all those years she was constantly moved around their palatial Derbyshire homes. She was imprisoned five times at Chatsworth House.

The royal status of the captive queen assured her of considerable privileges, except for the one thing she wanted most – freedom to wander around out of doors. As a slight concession, a belvedere was built in the grounds near the River Derwent. This single storey structure with blank stone walls is topped with a flat roof surrounded by a wall, broken in places by stone balustrading. The design is rather like a raised play-pen where the captive Queen could wonder to while away those long summer days. It was used for picnics as well as providing a grandstand for any entertainment in the grounds, but its main purpose as a prison was never in doubt. As a further precautionary step, the whole was surrounded by a moat and entered by a steep flight of stone steps. The design of this moated belvedere allowed Mary to spend considerable time in the open while still enclosed behind restricting walls with a substantial locked door or gate over which were Mary's initials and coat of arms.

Writing in '*The Estate – A View from Chatsworth*'the Dowager Duchess of Devonshire explains that the raised enclosure was built on the site of an ancient earthwork and adds – The building itself was largely restored by Wyatville in 1823-4 but its old bones are clearly visible in the thick walls and the broad flight of steps over the now dry moat.'

To mark the 400th anniversary of the death of Bess of Hardwick, the

bower was opened for daylight viewing in 2008, so I felt very privileged to be allowed to walk around the top, the entire surface of which is covered in meadow grass.

I was able to look out over the stone balustrade which documents date from 1581, and although the views are striking, the trees are now much too large to enjoy the same panorama that the Elizabethan visitors could. An added bonus was that all the recent rain had filled the moat.

Although I was aware that Mary Queen of Scots' unhappy spirit is said to walk around the area immediately in front of the building before ascending the steps and disappearing, sadly I didnt see her.

Apparently the ill fated Queen is seen surrounded by an azure light and always has a dejected look about her.

Does the ghost of Mary Queen of Scots haunt the bower?

Leave Queen Mary's Bower, and proceed to the haunted bridge over the River Derwent – 8. Millions of people pass over this stone bridge leading to Chatsworth House without really noticing it. Photographers walk slightly upstream to photograph the bridge with Chatsworth House in the background, but few give even a cursory glance at the other side where two stone statues adorn it. They are hardly a matching pair – one is a man holding a child on his shoulders, the other a classic

The view up river from the raised bower

male statue. The latter replaced a statue of a woman that fell into the water and was never retrieved, which is a shame because the original statues were said to be a sad reminder of a dreadful deed that happened in the 18th century.

Two servants working at Chatsworth House formed a liaison which blossomed into full union. The girl Frances Coulton became pregnant and gave birth to a baby boy. Immediately after the birth, the father James Loton of Edensor appeared on the scene, swept the new-born infant into his arms and ran towards the river. Pursued by the distraught mother, he paused at the bridge crossing the River Derwent, then threw the babe into the water.

According to a report at the time – *In March 22nd 1739, James Loton was found guilty at Derbyshire Assizes of the murder of a male bastard child. Frances Coulton gave evidence against him, because charged with the same offence, she turned King's evidence and was accordingly acquitted. Lord Chief Baron Page sentenced Loton to be hanged, but no fewer than six times over the following months, his sentence was respited. Accounts of the trial stated that he was a man of good standing, and probably more relevant under the circumstances, he was a man of considerable substance.*

Finally in August, he was eventually given a pardon and allowed to return home.
   But the crime is not totally forgotten, as the bridge has a reputation of being haunted. Walkers have been stopped in their tracks by the agonizing cries of the young mother who is said to haunt the bridge and river banks searching for her newborn child. What is equally distressing are the claims of people who have reported the gurgling gasps of the drowning baby.

Leave the bridge and turn towards Chatsworth House. At a fork of roads, take the left-hand fork to walk up to the entrance of Chatsworth House and Chatsworth stables which now house a couple of very nice restaurants and craft shops. A few hours spent here is highly recommended.

The haunted bridge
with Chatsworth House behind

Although there appears to be no record of any actual ghosts at Chatsworth House, it is just the kind of place where you would expect to find spectres gliding along corridors and down grand staircases, and you wouldnt be disappointed. Ghostly ladies have been seen, but as the history of Chatsworth House has been shaped by so many famous and tragic figures, it is difficult to pinpoint which specific spirit presence might be hanging around. Doors have been seen to open and close by themselves. Footsteps, muffled voices, banging, clattering and thumping noises have been heard.
   The present Dowager Duchess has experienced several phantoms within the building and in the library, is said to have watched an opaque phantom glide about the room. The spirit presence of an older lady with an autocratic manner has been felt, and this is believed to be Evelyn, the wife of the 9th Duke of Devonshire. A very talented needlewoman, for fifty years, the Duchess carefully restored many rare embroideries and tapestries, and now her ghost is said to still be taking the responsibility of caring for Chatsworth very seriously.

To continue our walk, cross a cattle grid and pass Chatsworth Farmyard – 9 – on your left. Follow the estate road as it bears right up through the woods signed 'Stand Wood Walks'. After about 100 metres opposite an old building and just before four coloured arrows on a low stone on the left-hand side of the road, leave the road and turn left up a narrow woodland path through the laurels and rhododendrons. Cross another wider track diagonally left and continue up the winding, narrow path, crossing a stream and walking round a large Yew tree to the steps.

Climb the 148 steps to the Hunting Tower – 10. It was previously called Stand Tower and was built in 1582 in order to watch the hounds hunting in the valley below. The woods covering the hillside behind Chatsworth House are known as Stand Wood. Stand means a place of height for spectators, hence 'grandstand' at a sports arena. The canon at the base of the Hunting Tower came from a ship that fought at the Battle of Trafalgar.

Turn left to follow the road round the tower on the track signposted Robin Hood. Isn't this just the kind of place you might expect to encounter the famous outlaw?

At a crossing of roads turn left on a surfaced road through the woods. After about ½ mile, the road bends right up to a large shed. Keep straight on along a farm track for a few metres then just before a gateway turn left

The Hunting Tower was previously called Stand Tower and was built in 1582

through the wood. Follow the wall on your right. Cross the high wall stile, turn right then left to follow the wall on your right. After about 300 metres and before the wall corner, the path bears left to cross another high stile. Keep straight on up the field to walk along the concessionary path of Dobb Edge – 11. Cross the stile in the field corner. Follow the narrow, winding, rocky path as it undulates. Cross two stiles and after about 400 metres at the end of Dobb Edge, cross a ladder stile. Over to your right is Gibbet Wood and behind that is Gibbet Moor so listen hard!

Bear left down hill following the way marked post and crossing a wider track. Go down steps to cross a planked bridge over Heathy Lea Brook then climb the steps to the A619 road. Cross the road and turn right to return to Robin Hood, the start/end of this walk.

Does the famous outlaw haunt the hamlet of Robin Hood?

9: Demons, Witches, Hobs and Headless Coffin Bearers

White Lodge Car Park – Demons Dale – Monsal Dale – Monsal Head – Little Longstone – Thornbridge Hall – Monsal Trail – Ashford in the Water –Great Shacklow Wood – White Lodge
6½ Miles (10·5km)

Thousands of people visit Monsal Head to admire the view down into the Wye Valley. It must be one of the finest and best known in England and not only does our walk incorporate this, it also includes three very attractive, typically English villages separated by lovely and varied countryside. The first stage is through Demons Dale where the sensitives amongst you might experience a strange atmosphere. There are demons, fairies and hobs for starters and as the walk continues we might encounter the witches of Monsal Dale, twelve headless men carrying a coffin and other ghostly tales.

Our walk begins at the White Lodge Pay & Display Car Park on the A6. From Bakewell, take the A6 north through Ashford in the Water and after almost 3½ miles (5.3km), the car park is on your left.

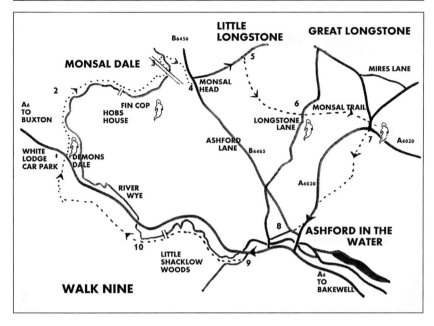

THE WALK

Leave the car park – 1 – by walking past the pay and display machine on your left and down three steps which drop straight onto the A6. Cross the road and go through the stile on the opposite side and down five steps. Follow the well defined path through a field, to cross stepping stones and a stile, and enter a wood. A wood is a lonely place at the best of times, and in the dim and distant past, landscape features were often named in recognition of the characters that resided there, so when I tell you that this wood borders a valley named Demon's Dale, you may detect a certain distinct eeriness about the place.

According to a book called the Itinerarum, a literary work by a 15th century writer called William Worcester – *'the River Wye runs through a valley called Dymynsdale, (Demon's Dale) where spirits are tortured and souls are tormented'*. Even allowing for a bit of artistic licence, that's pretty heavy stuff for such a beautiful, tranquil spot.

If you're brave enough to continue, ignore the branch paths and head for the river and Monsal Dale. In the elbow of a bend of the river you'll find a weathered limestone crag which is supposedly the petrified remains of the leader of a race of giants who once lived in the recesses of Demon's Dale. Locals give it wide berth and even now adhere to the old superstition of spitting when passing in the belief that this will stop any force of evil coming from the rock and attaching itself to the traveller. Spitting was regularly employed to repel witch-craft or the evil eye, or to ensure good luck, but concern for hygiene and good manners make it rare now. There are still examples of people spitting on coins for luck, or spitting on their hands before a fight or hard manual work, and in *Walk 2* we encounter a spitting ghost.

The petrified remains of Hulac Warren in the bend of the river

So who was this leader of giants who was turned to stone? According to the legend, his name was Hulac Warren and he lusted after a young shepherdess named Hedessa, but she resisted all his advances. Hulac Warren refused to take no for an answer and although he soon realised that he stood no chance of winning her affections by fair means, he was prepared to use foul. He was accustomed to having his

A giant of a man sprang out of the bushes and grabbed her

own way and he intended to have Hedessa whether she was in agreement or not, but the gods watched Hulac and they were not pleased. They tried to protect the young girl who was pure, kind and loving but it was inevitable that one evening as Hedessa returned home through the valley of Demon Dale, Hulac saw his chance. He sprang up from the bushes where he had been hiding and grabbed her.

Hedessa fought bravely, but he was giant of a man and it was soon evident that her struggles were in vain. In desperation she called out to the gods for help. They heard her plea and momentarily stunned Hulac, allowing Hedessa to escape from his grasp.

Hedessa ran as fast as she could, but Hulac was soon in hot pursuit and gaining fast. In desperation, she ran towards a rocky precipice and threw herself to her death. As she fell, fragments of the rock also broke away and on the ground below, they formed a protective circle around her body, securing it from anything unclean. Almost immediately, a spring of pure water, as untainted as Hedessas soul sprang from the limestone rocks weeping sad symbolic tears in mourning for the lovely shepherdess.

Hulac Warren was furious at being robbed of the chance of possessing Hedessa and cursed the gods for interfering. This enraged the gods who sent a mighty gale which blew him off the rocks into the river, and there he still lies in his petrified state, waist deep in chilly water paying an eternal penance.

The path – 2 – runs on the left of the river for about a mile, and the vista becomes glorious as the river rounds the foot of Fin Cop which was a prehistoric hill fort.

Over on your right is Hobs House, a weird assemblage of rocks with an unsavoury reputation, and a hill called Great Fin noted for the very green spots that dot its slopes. Our ancestors believed that these were fairy rings, owing their greenness to the moonlight revels of the little people. Many sightings were alleged of fairies dressed in green, dancing hand in hand around their rings to the music of the field cricket, grasshopper or drone bee, aided in their joyous movements by the light of numerous glow-worms. William Shakespeare alluded to such widespread beliefs in many of his plays and from The Tempus comes the lines –

'Ye elves – ye demy puppets, that by moonshine do the green-sour ringlets make.'

> The presence of fungi and mushrooms is the real, if rather less notable cause of the greenness of fairy rings and in Derbyshire, young mushrooms are still known as fairy buttons. When they begin to decay, local lore acknowledges that the devil has been at work on them and driven out the fairies.

Ahead of you is the stone railway viaduct – 3, its huge arches rising 80ft above the river. When erected in Monsal Dale by the Midland Railway in 1862-3 it roused the wrath of John Ruskin who wrote – *'That valley where you might expect to catch sight of Pan, Apollo and the Muses, is now desecrated in order that a Buxton fool may be able to find himself in Bakewell at the end of twelve minutes and vice versa.'* As a focal point, how well it now blends into the landscape.

On approaching the viaduct – 3, pass through a squeeze stile by a gate and walk under the viaduct to continue along the riverside path. In about 200 yards turn right to cross the footbridge over the River Wye and continue along the opposite bank past a weir.

> For many centuries, belief in witchcraft was a major element of country life. Wise men and witches were a regular feature of village and small town life and although not well documented, we know that at Monsal Dale lived Betty Higgins and her father Neddy who were known as the witches of Monsal Dale. Betty and Neddy Higgins sold rags to make a living but supplemented their income by divining the future, selling cures, charms, love magic, potions and nostrums. They were consulted to help locate lost or stolen property, or in William Cundy's case, – *see Walk 7* to find a
>
> 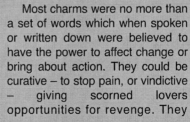 missing child. These were the stock in trade of all witches.
>
> Most charms were no more than a set of words which when spoken or written down were believed to have the power to affect change or bring about action. They could be curative – to stop pain, or vindictive – giving scorned lovers opportunities for revenge. They

were so generally and thoroughly accepted that even medical men believed in their efficiency. When written down they would be worn sewn into the necks of coats or into the waistbands of petticoats – see the story of Ellen Gregory of Over Haddon in *Walk 1*.

To continue our walk, keep on the path as it climbs steadily through woodlands until you reach steps which take you up to Monsal Head – 4. After the exertion, turn and enjoy the view over the valley. This is a good spot for a break at the Monsal Head Hotel or at Hobbs Café and Craft shop. There's a Hobbs ice-cream van too.

The view down into Monsal Dale and the viaduct that infuriated John Ruskin

From Monsal Head the routes are clearly signposted

Leave Monsal head and cross the B6465 road to walk down the opposite road to Little Longstone – 5. The road falls gently eastward past the 19th century congregational chapel, before dipping into a tree lined hollow beside a terrace of charming limestone cottages and the ancient ivy covered Packhorse Inn. This area was rich in mineral deposits, so its not surprising to find that this was originally built in the late 16th century as two lead miners cottages and converted in 1787 to an inn. Longstone Moor is criss-crossed with old pack horse routes, used now only for recreational purposes, but the inn has retained its original name for over 200 years.

A few yards after passing the Packhorse Inn on your left, on your right is the village spring and the site of the annual Little Longstone well-dressing which combines the date with its larger neighbour at Great Longstone. If you are able to visit during these well-dressing festivities, one form of entertainment you might encounter is Morris Dancing and a group calling themselves Freaks in the Peaks. Characterised by energy and enthusiasm, this mixed group of dancers and musicians perform their own interpretation of traditional Morris Dances in the same way that they were originally performed by seasonally unemployed workmen. As this was considered a form of begging and therefore illegal, it was necessary to entertain the public in disguise, a tradition which the Freaks in the Peaks still maintain.

Freaks in the Peaks perform Border Morris dances

After passing Manor Farm Cottages on your left, you will reach the imposing Little Longstone Manor, home for 800 years of the Longsden family. Almost opposite is The Hollow, now run by Dawn Gregory, who offers bed and breakfast. Just past is a combination of gates and stiles signed Ashford and Monsal Trail. An equally old building called The Stocks with a date stone of 1575 lies a few yards down the road on the left.

*To follow the path
from Little Longstone,
go through the gate,
over the wall,
or through the stile*

Go straight on across two fields and through two gates then follow the path and the wall up the third field to cross a stile on your right. Turn left along the Monsal Trail, the eight and a half mile route between Bakewell and Chee Dale, of the former Midland Railway Line. The route has been graded and turned into a walk way for the public and a haven for nature, and its now hard to image that before 1968, this track was wide enough to carry mainline trains thundering along in both directions.

140

A handbill from July 1962 encouraging people to use the train that ran along this track to reach their walking destination. The fare from Derby to Great Longstone was 6s 6d (32½p)

On this first section of the walk, the banking rises on both sides, until you reach Great Longstone Station which is one of the highlights of this stretch of the Monsal Trail. The Victorian Station Masters House, full of charm and character is now privately owned, but the raised station platforms on both sides are still intact. The actual station was at one stage going to be called Thornbridge because from the platform rises a flight of steps to the garden gate of Thornbridge Hall. This rather imposing stone building was erected by a Victorian industrialist and later became a teacher's training collage. This part is now Thornbridge Outdoors, a conference centre run by Sheffield City Centre providing training courses, outdoor and environmental activities.

Advertising Seeing Derbyshire By Train

Part of Thornbridge Hall estate stands on the side of the Monsal Trail

On your left, just before the railway bridge and directly opposite the station building, take a short diversion by climbing the steps up to the road. At the top turn right over the bridge and walk for about 100 yards down the lane towards the gates of Thornbridge Hall.

This is Shady Lane, a rather lonely stretch of road which runs between Great Longstone and Ashford in the Water, but supposedly if you travel along here at dusk or dawn you may encounter twelve men carrying a coffin. On closer inspection you will see that the men are headless and the coffin empty, apparently intended for the unfortunate person who meets this strange funeral cortege.

However, take heart, I'm assured that people have seen this strange procession and lived to tell the tale. If the funeral cortege are walking towards you it means you will be scooped up into the coffin, but if they are walking away, you will be fine. I'm not sure what would happen if you made the split second decision to turn and ran which would surely be the most obvious solution!

Return to the Monsal Trail and continue under the railway bridge.

The view looking back through the railway bridge
with the station building on the left

After about another half a mile it is time to leave the Monsal Trail. After passing a bench and a footpath sign down to Great Longstone which goes across the fields, the Monsal Trail crosses a road bridge. Just after, there's a path on the left which drops down onto the road at the junction of roads to Hassop and Great Longstone. Ignore these and turn left to walk under the bridge you have just walked over. On your right are more impressive gates leading to Thornbridge Hall and in a few yards the road joins the A6020 at a grass triangle.

The road joins the A6020,
and our path goes up the lane opposite between the trees

Go straight ahead across the A6020 and walk up the tree lined, minor road signed 'Private No Parking' and 'Public Footpath'. Follow this road for nearly half a mile passing Churchdale Lodge and at the entrance to Churchdale Hall, bear left to cross a ladder stile on the right of a metal gate.

Keep straight on following the boundary wall of Churchdale Hall on your right and the ha-ha in front of the hall. Cross the stile by a stand of trees. Bear very slightly left across the middle of the field to cross a fence stile. Continue in the same direction to cross another fence stile. Follow a path downhill through the trees to go through a small gate and across a stream then on up to go through a squeeze stile.

Turn left along the A6020 and at the road junction, turn right into the village. The next stretch through Ashford in the Water is shared with *Walk 10*.

We are entering Ashford in the Water on the B6465, Greave Lane where you will find a building named Candle House. Greaves is the name given to the waste tallow from candle manufacture and would indicate that in pre-electricity days, when most villages were self-sufficient, candles were made here. Follow the road round to the left into Church Street. Half way along on your left is Great Batch Hall and the Church of The Holy Trinity (see *walk 10* for more information). Continue to the end of Church Street dominated by the octagonal shelter built to commemorate the Queen's Silver Jubilee 1952-1977, turn left and at the end of the lane is sheep wash bridge built in the 17th century and near the site of the original ford which gave Ashford its name.

Cross the sheep wash bridge with its sheep pen over the River Wye and turn right down the A6 for 250 metres, then cross the road and turn left at the sign for Sheldon. Stay on the road for about 325 metres and where the road starts to climb and bend left, bear right off the road down a short track to go through a small gate.

Follow the riverside path for just over ½ mile with the river on your right crossing two stiles and ignoring all side paths. On reaching a small bridge and old mill buildings turn left to walk up passing to the left of the buildings. Continue along the pretty undulating, winding path through Great Shacklow Wood, at first level then climbing upwards for about ¾ mile ignoring all side paths. Cross a stile over a wall. The path then starts to drop down and you leave the woods. A little further you will come to a bridleway sign to A6 and White Lodge where you cross a stile and turn right. Go down this rocky path, crossing two stiles until you reach White Lodge Car Park which is the start/end of this walk.

10: Bagpipes, Ducks and Ghostly Miners

BAKEWELL – ASHFORD IN THE WATER
– SHELDON – MAGPIE MINE
Distance 7½ Miles (12·15km)

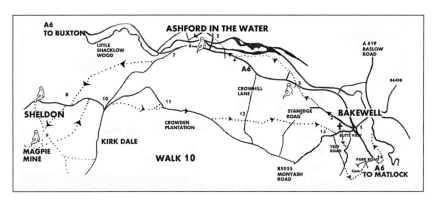

Walk Ten begins at Bakewell – 1, so park in any of the pay and display car-parks and make your way to Rutland Square. Facing the Rutland Hotel, cross the road and go up North Church Street. The Church is on your left as you walk up the hill. It turns sharply right and continues to rise as it turns left then right again. Stay on this road past St Anselms School on your right – 2. This is where a photograph taken in the grounds showed a Victorian child had unexpectedly appeared in the group.

Just after the school buildings, turn right at the footpath sign for Ashford. Bear left to another footpath sign and cross the playing field at the bottom of a steep bank to a third footpath sign and a track into Endcliffe Woods. The path drops steeply down to the A6 Buxton Road next to Deepdale Business Park – 3.

145

> When looking for a property to buy in Bakewell, I looked at many houses including one in this area. As I was shown round, I could distinctly hear bagpipes being played. As it seemed very distant and indistinct, I decided it must be coming from the radio or TV of a neighbouring property. It wasnt until years later I discovered that the previous occupants had been in a Scottish dancing troupe and the gentleman actually played the bagpipes. Had the sound of his practicing somehow become imprinted in the fabric of the property?

Cross the road, turn left and after a short distance turn right through a stile by the gate. Cross the field on a path between wall and fence, then cross the road called Lakeside. Continue on a narrow fenced path, then a well defined path that runs parallel to the river, with spectacular views of the weirs along the way. Stay on this path until reaching a footpath sign leading you back on to the A6 Buxton Road – 4. Turn right and walk along the road until reaching a lane on the right. This is now closed to traffic, but its possible to park at either end. Cross two bridges and note the date and initials on the second bridge – M Hyde 1664. According to the story, the Reverend Hyde, vicar of Bakewell was riding over the bridge when his horse took fright and jumped over the parapet, killing them both.

The letters chiselled in the stone bridge remind us that the Rev. M. Hyde was killed here in 1664

Keep straight ahead to reach the A6020 road. Cross over and bear slightly right up the B6465 into the village of Ashford in the Water – 5. The village grew up around the ford over the River Wye on the

Portway, the ancient route that we've also encountered in *Walk 3* and *Walk 6*. It was used as a major crossing point of the River Wye for pack-horse trains carrying malt from Derby, and up to 300 pack horses would have crossed the River Wye here every week. A mill and a lead mine were recorded under Aisseford in the Domesday Book and Ashford remained a centre of the lead mining industry until the late 19th century. One hundred and fifty years ago, the villagers worked on the land, in the mines or at one of the water-powered mills that cut and polished Ashford marble.

Ashford marble is a dark, fine grained limestone which occurs in the west of Ashford at Rookery Wood, takes on a jet-black gloss when polished. Examples of this can be found in the fireplaces at Hardwick Hall and the private chapel at Chatsworth House but the most spectacular pieces of Ashford marble are those that have been painstakingly inlaid with floral arrangements and geometric shapes cut from other sources of local, coloured varieties of limestone and fluorspar. From Nettler Dale in Sheldon comes rosewood which produced the effect of grained wood when polished. From Monyash came a mottled and veined limestone varying in tint from faint blue to azure-purple. Different shades of barytes occur at Arbor Low, Bradwell and Castleton. Wetton and Sheldon provide a fossil bearing rock cut to present cross-sections of crinoids – fossilised marine organisms. This inlay work required a painstaking skill that rivalled Italian craftsmanship to produce trinkets and jewellery, paperweights and ornaments. There is a fine selection in Buxton Museum and Art Gallery, and a prize-winning table dating from 1882 in the church at Ashford In The Water.

We are entering Ashford in the Water on the B6465, Greave Lane where you will find a building named Candle House. Greaves is the name given to the waste tallow from candle manufacture and would indicate that in pre-electricity days, when most villages were self-sufficient, candles were made here.

Follow the road round to the left into Church Street. Half way along on your left is Great Batch Hall.

In the Oak room at Great Batch Hall, the timber chimney breast bears the imprint of a duck. How it got there is a story that dates back to the 17th century and is told later. Great Batch Hall is also reputed to be haunted although the ghost is, I'm assured, a benign one.

Great Batch Hall is haunted by a benign ghost

On your right is the Church of the Holy Trinity. The original building was Norman but it was almost entirely rebuilt in 1870. A visit is a must to not only see the rare and exquisite inlaid table mentioned previously, this is one of the few churches where it is still possible to see Virgin Crants suspended.

Also known as Maiden's Garlands or Crowns, these are now very rare examples of the sad, commemorative garlands that were carried at the funeral of a young girl, then left suspended over the family pew. This is a tradition that dates back to at least Elizabethan times and even Shakespeare refers to it.

The Church of the Holy Trinity, where five rare virgin crants are suspended

Continue to the end of Church Street dominated by the octagonal shelter built to commemorate the Queen's Silver Jubilee 1952-1977.

Turn left and at the end of the lane is sheep wash bridge built in the 17th century and near the site of the original ford which gave Ashford its name. This bridge is unusual in that it has a stone walled enclosure incorporated into the structure, large enough to hold a folk of sheep. Until recently, sheep were brought here to be washed in the river before being sheared. The ewes with halters round their necks, were pushed into the river, ducked and made to swim downstream to re-join their lambs on the bank, and at the far end there's a pen which was used when washing sheep in the river. The wool trade has thrived in Derbyshire for hundreds of years and sheep dipping was an annual event because cleaner fleeces meant higher prices.

The Sheepwash Bridge with its unusual pen incorporated into the wall

Cross the sheep wash bridge to the A6 at an area known as Duke's Drive – 6. Two Dukes are prominent landowners in this area, the Duke of Devonshire and the Duke of Rutland. An ancestor of the latter, Sir George Vernon was also given the rather grand title King of the Peak.

Sir George Vernon has gone down in history as the last Vernon of Haddon Hall, see *Walk 2*, and the father of the eloping heiress Dorothy, so how did he earn this title? According to the writings of Stephen Glover in 1830, it was because of his generous hospitality and almost royal life-style, yet it is more likely to be another reason, his indulgence in the 'Lynch Law'. When the body of a peddler who had been in the area selling his wares was found, it looked like murder, so George Vernon ordered every servant and villager to touch the body in turn. This was known as ordeal by touch and the guilty party was believed to shed blood when he touched the body. When one cottager refused and ran, this was seen as guilt. George Vernon immediately ordered his men to give chase and they finally caught him at Ashford in the Water where George Vernon took the law into his own hands and without a trial, hanged the man in a field.

Only the King of England, under exceptional circumstances was allowed to do this, and although Sir George Vernon did stand trial for his action, the indictment was in the name of 'King of the Peak' and he was acquitted. From that day on, the field became known as Lynch Field or Gallows Acre.

Turn right and cross the road, turning left at the road sign to Sheldon – 7. Stay on this road until reaching a footpath on your right where you leave the road to go through a stile by the side of a gate. Take the left branch which rises to a wall where you turn left, following the directions of the arrow signs. This is an area of deep valleys and rounded hills criss-

A humorous sign with a serious message

crossed by dry-stone walls. The path goes up by the wall on your right, before zigzagging round to reach another footpath marker. Sheep are plentiful here.

Continue ahead on this path, on the left side of a broken wall, towards Little Shacklow Woods. Continue on the left side of Little Shacklow Woods then go across the fields until reaching a stile on your left at the road. Turn right to take you into Sheldon – 8, an attractive village mentioned in the Domesday Book, where a distinctive fossil bearing rock is produced. Could this have been the inspiration for our next story?

According to folklore, in 1601, villagers in Sheldon saw a duck fly into an ash tree and disappear. For the next three centuries this was known as the Duck Tree, then it was felled and cut into planks. Much to their surprise, an unmistakable imprint the size and shape of a duck was obvious between the centre two planks of wood. The timber merchant was so impressed, he had the planks cut and polished and set into a mantelpiece at his home, Great Batch Hall.

Sheldon has a single village street with stone-built cottages and farms behind a series of linear village greens, an important landscape feature in this street scene. The buildings date mainly from the 18th century when lead mining was prosperous and like many of the villages around this area, Sheldon owes much to its lead mining industry. Even before the Roman invasion, lead was being mined here, but the industry was at its height in the 17th and 18th centuries. During the second half of the 19th century, richer and cheaper lead reserves were found elsewhere, and as these supplies flooded the market, Derbyshire lead became uneconomical and the industry went into sharp decline. The last big mine closed in 1939 bringing to an end over 2,000 years of lead mining, leaving just the workings and spoil heaps – 'lead rakes' – as an important reminder of our heritage.

The village inn, the Cock and Pullett, is typical of the stone cottages on Sheldon's main street

There are a number of footpaths that leave Sheldon to converge at Magpie Mine. Just after the 30 mile speed limit sign at the top of the hill, turn left at the footpath sign. Take this broad track through an iron gate and continue straight ahead through three fields with a wall on your right. Go over the stile into the fourth field with the wall now on your left. Turn left at the footpath sign and head diagonally across the field towards Magpie Mine – 9 which stands on the hills above the village of Sheldon.

Derbyshire lead miners

An Artist's impression of Magpie Mine in operation

Magpie Mine is one of the best preserved lead mines in the area whose surface works have been restored as a visitor attraction. It was worked for over 300 years from the early 17th century, but had a very troubled past. Lead miners were a pugnacious breed who would fight bitterly for their rights, so when in 1824, tunnels from the Magpie Mine and the adjacent Red Soil Mine ran close together and merged, disputes over the lead-bearing veins were inevitable. This difference of opinion lasted for several years during which time there was fighting and vandalism, then tragedy

Magpie Mine, now one of the best preserved lead mines in the country

occurred when the miners tried to smoke each other out. Three miners died of asphyxiation in 1833 and it is said that their widows put a curse on the mine.

Miners, like many others who work in hazardous occupations were greatly influenced by superstition, and the curse was taken very seriously. From that point on until its closure in 1926, the Magpie Mine had a history of flooding, fires, hauntings and roof-falls and the miners believed these to be signs that should be heeded. Is that why it was named Magpie – traditionally a bird of ill omen?

Even though it is no longer worked, people believe that it is haunted by the old miners who still frequent the Magpie Mine. It is said that if you stand at the top of the old shaft, you can hear the ghostly voices of the long-dead miners calling in the galleries below.

In 1946, a party of speleologists were exploring the Magpie Mine when one of them saw a man with a candle walking along the tunnel, before suddenly disappearing. The apparition was dismissed as imagination until the photographs from the mine were developed and showed that another member of the party was standing on a raft in a flooded sough accompanied by a second figure standing on top of eight foot of water.

Leave the Magpie Mine and head N.NE to Johnson Lane. Follow this east to the staggered cross road at Kirk Dale – 10, taking the footpath opposite, past Dirtlow Plantation to Dirtlow Farm to where it reaches the lane – 11. Walk straight ahead veering slightly right and follow the road past Crowden Plantations until reaching a footpath on your left.

Climb down some steps and cross five fields divided by hawthorne hedges, following the track until reaching Crowhill Lane – 12. Cross

An artist's impression of the church and old cottages opposite Butts View

the lane and continuing in the same direction walk down the left of the field. Pass through a wicket gate in the corner then veer right descend into a grassy valley and rise out of it to follow the path with the copse of trees on your left and head uphill until reaching Stanedge Road. Turn left for 10 yards then enter a field. Stay in the same direction through four fields to arrive at a footpath between Thorncliffe and The Orchard on Parsonage Croft, Bakewell – 13. Go slightly right onto South Church Street, cross the B5055 Monyash Road and walk down until reaching Butts View on your right.

The name butts indicates the old practice of archery. In medieval times, the law dictated that every able-bodied man had to be proficient at archery, and straw butts were set up on suitable ground to enable men to practice. This land became known as The Butts or in this case, Butts View, Butts Terrace and Butts Road.

From Butts View take a footpath through to Butts Road. Turn right. Go round the left bend and on to the T junction with Calton View. Turn left into Burton Edge and continue past the gates of the cemetery. As the road veers right, follow the unsurfaced lane straight ahead beside the wall of the cemetery until reaching a double footpath sign opposite tennis courts. Straight on would go to Youlgreave, but turn left along the narrow footpath between the wall and hedge, still skirting the cemetery on your left. Follow this footpath going down steps through Catcliffe Woods into Park View. Turn left, then at the junction, turn right down to the main A6 Matlock Road. Cross the road, turn right and after 100 yards enter the recreation ground – 14.

The track goes alongside the cemetery

Just inside the gate you will encounter a small pond, the only evidence of the spring which used to feed the recently removed children's paddling pool. Like the spring water that

154

was obtained from the wells in the centre see *Walk 1*, this was also a chalybeate spring known as Peat Well, probably a corruption of St Peter's Well, with waters at 56 degrees F. The notice board claims it is Holywell but sadly, it is very shabby and too difficult to read.

Go along the path round the children's recreation area towards the river then keep to the river path back to Bakewell which is the start/end of this walk.

Looking rather sad and neglected, the only evidence of Bakewell's St Peter's Well in the recreation ground

GHOST WALKS OF BRITAIN

1: GHOST WALKS IN AND AROUND BAKEWELL

Titles in preparation

GHOST WALKS IN AND AROUND CHESTERFIELD

GHOST WALKS IN AND AROUND THE DEAD CENTRE

GHOST WALKS IN AND AROUND DERBY

GHOST WALKS IN AND AROUND EYAM

FOLKLORE IN ENGLAND

1: CUSTOMS IN KENT

2: CUSTOMS IN YORKSHIRE

Titles in preparation

CUSTOMS IN CORNWALL

CUSTOMS IN DERBYSHIRE

CUSTOMS IN DEVON

CUSTOMS IN EAST ANGLIA

CUSTOMS IN LONDON